Best Answers to the 201 Most Frequently Asked Interview Questions

Other books by Matthew J. DeLuca

How to Find a Job in 90 Days or Less: A Realistic Action Plan for Finding the Right Job Fast, 1995

Best Answers to the 201 Most Frequently Asked Interview Questions

Matthew J. DeLuca

McGraw-Hill

New York   San Francisco   Washington, D.C.   Auckland   Bogotá
Caracas   Lisbon   London   Madrid   Mexico City   Milan
Montreal   New Delhi   San Juan   Singapore
Sydney   Tokyo   Toronto

McGraw-Hill

*A Division of The **McGraw·Hill** Companies*

18 19 20   QWF/QWF   0 7 6 5 4 3

ISBN 0-07-016357-X

The sponsoring editor for this book was Betsy N. Brown, the editing supervisor was Penny Linskey, and the production supervisor was Suzanne W. B. Rapcavage. It was set in Palatino by Inkwell Publishing Services.

Contents

Preface

This book is intended to be used to enhance your job search efforts either as a stand-alone product or in combination with *How to Find a Job in 90 Days or Less,* also by Matt DeLuca. The emphasis of this book is on the dynamics of the interview—an essential component of any job search effort. *How to Find a Job in 90 Days or Less* takes a broader approach and emphasizes the steps required to launch a successful job hunting campaign and to take it to its successful conclusion.

The approach of both books is practical and hands-on. You should do more than just read the book. *Use it* by practicing its suggestions—do what it asks you to do with a friend, family member, or colleague. Practice answering the questions peppered throughout the book, not so that you memorize the answers and recite them by rote, but rather so that you can listen to yourself and, in the process, determine what works and what doesn't. The result is that, when you go to the interview and are asked these questions or others like them, you will be totally prepared and effective.

But perhaps the interview is in the morning, and this is the first time you have had to look for a job in years. The author has made an attempt to help someone like you who needs to fly through the book and get help fast. Look for questions with a star (☆) next to them. These questions, I feel, are the most likely to be asked and will help you to be the most prepared in the shortest time—regardless of what questions are actually asked during the interview.

Acknowledgments

Any book requires the support and assistance of a variety of individuals that, in combination, lead to the completion of the project. At the top of my list is my extremely talented colleague, friend, and wife, Nanette, who is becoming a more essential element of these projects with each project undertaken. Although not always in agreement, she certainly provides invaluable assistance in taking my ideas and making them a coherent and complete manuscript.

Also to be mentioned are Lisa Wolf, a terrific professional and a great fan, as well as Palma Mitchell, a solid human resource expert and a lot more. Also to be mentioned are the executives and employees at a unique organization—Titan Sports, Inc.—in particular Vince and Linda McMahon, as well as Dawn Lyon, all of whom have been great to work with and have helped me to gain additional insight on many job searches from a recruiter's perspective in a most challenging environment. Last let me mention my friends and colleagues at New York University, among whom I want to mention Lynn Johnson and Ken Coleman (and the deceased LeVaun Eustice, before them), who have provided me with a great educational setting in which to grow professionally and an ongoing forum to develop new approaches to a variety of human resource issues, including recruiting, and test them in the marketplace.

Last, let me thank the people at McGraw-Hill for all their interest and attention. At the top of the list is Philip Ruppel for guiding me through this aspect of my career and for what has become my sixth book. Thanks to Betsy Brown for, one more time, taking me through the steps from book concept and proposal to its successful conclusion. And to Fred Dahl for a painstaking editing of the manuscript.

MATTHEW J. DELUCA

List of Questions

Best Answers
to the
201 Most
Frequently
Asked
Interview
Questions

1

Introduction

What This Book Does for You

This book prepares you for the most important aspect of the job search: *how to answer the toughest job interview questions effectively.* These all-important interviews are a major part of the process. **Remember: the best candidates don't necessarily get the job: the best interviewee does.** The candidate who best handles the recruitment and selection process of the organization is the one ultimately chosen.

With finding a job growing more difficult each day, this book specifically identifies opportunities for you to shine during the interview process—opportunities that position you in the most favorable light and increase your prospects each and every time.

The goal is a straightforward one: to identify major questions as part of the preparation process, so that when you are called on, you're ready with the right answer—not with memorized responses but with informed, reasoned replies. What this book does for you is to prepare you for the job process and eminently for the arduous aspects of interviewing. Remember, the best resume does not land the job. It is very possible for a person to get a job without a resume, but rarely does a person get a job without an effective interview. This is true for most positions in most occupations and becomes increasingly true the higher up a person proceeds through the organizational hierarchy regardless of the sector: private, not-for-profit, and government.

To prepare for the best interview possible, you need to have great answers to a broad range of questions. To help you, this book is broken down into various categories of questions as follows:

Decide which areas you need the most help on and tackle those first. Where do your strengths lie? Are you a great manager but your technical skills are a bit rusty? Go to Education and Experience questions first to look for "sales points" to stress. If you have been locked up doing research for the past two years, your "personal" area may need attention. Leave none to chance. Do not avoid illegal and small talk questions. A review of those questions may provide more consideration than you had thought necessary and build your confidence in the other broad topic areas.

The goal is to prepare you so that you are sensitive to all the facets of the process and give the questions the attention they deserve. While concentrating on answering the interviewers' questions skillfully, you also need to stay alert to the nonverbal aspects of the communication process. You do this not just to land the job but also to determine whether you are interested in working at the interviewer's firm. Why prolong the interview process if you have negative vibes about the organization?

One last point about all these questions and soul searching: You may discover that you are lacking either skills and/or experience in certain areas. Start working on them now during your job search. Take a class, read books, get out and network with others in your profession, go to the library and do research, contact professional organizations to find out about meetings and membership. **Most job openings come from referrals. Make things happen for yourself. Get out and interact.** Interview others at meetings. With the possible exception of stressful job interviews, people love to talk about themselves. Try out some of the questions that trouble you. The more people who know that you are actively searching for a new job, the more chances you have to get lines on future interviews. **Follow the "arm's-length" rule: Everyone within arm's-length of you should know you are looking for a job.** You never know who may overhear your conversation while waiting in line at the theater, doing their laundry, or making a copy at the copy shop—and be able to refer you to a job opening. Just keep talking!

Difficulty of Finding a Job in This Market

Today's market is a particularly difficult one in which to obtain employment for a lot of reasons:

Time

To find the right person (or any person for that matter), the employer has to make a time and resource commitment. With continuous efforts to reduce staff, each organization appears to have fewer and fewer persons for all the tasks required. That is particularly true of professionals in the Personnel/Human Resource Department because that is usually the first one identified to reduce headcount.

Other factors further complicate the hiring process. When an organization reduces its staff, it loses the trained and skilled professionals who were responsible for screening candidates. Their knowledge and experience are "downsized" along with them.

Training

Is any required? For the applicant this becomes frustrating because, even though the openings are there, the organization is relying on more and more inexperienced (i.e., untrained) recruiters and interviewers who do not know what to look for. The result is that the wrong applicants are invited in and the wrong candidates are then hired.

To compound the problem, downsizing itself discounts the human element of the organization. There is an organizational disregard for human capital (most commonly referred to as an "expense") and for the organizational knowledge and unique experience of each terminated employee. New interviewers are given scant or no training because people are not highly regarded by many organizations, nor is the process of how they are brought into the organization.

Cost

Whenever there is an opening, there are direct and indirect costs in any hiring process.

❏ *Direct costs* are the most visible in the recruiting process. These include fees for placement, costs for ads placed in the papers, travel and entertainment expenses, and fees paid for tests.

❏ *Indirect costs* are not-so-visible costs that should be considered as well. The first is the lost opportunity cost that occurs due to the vacancy itself and the lost sales directly attributable to the lack of personnel. Other indirect costs include the time taken by any employee to recruit and interview each applicant, the time to train new people once on board, and the business lost waiting for a new employee to get up to speed and add value to the organization, or, in the case of an unsuccessful hire, business lost due to the new employee's ineffectiveness.

A "Buyer's Market"?

"There are a million applicants out there. It's a buyer's market." The media are chiefly responsible for this *unrealistic perception* of a huge surplus of talented people just waiting to be grabbed. The idea is that a low bid in this market is not only cost-effective, it is downright astute. One thing that fuels this widespread belief is the relatively high rate of unemployment, along with the continuous reporting of major organizations and their latest downsizing announcement.

Another contribution to this unrealistic perception has to do with the placement of classified ads. Talk to anyone who has done it and the superficially aware boast about the fact that they ran an ad in the paper for a position and garnered a huge number of resumes (400 seems to be the current magic number). But talk to those responsible for sifting through the 400 replies; if they get a single hire out of the process, they consider themselves lucky.

For the real lowdown, talk to Personnel/Human Resource professionals anywhere in the United States, and they will share with you a very different view. They will immediately agree that, if you run an ad for any position, you will be deluged with resumes by fax, mail, and phone. **The problem is that resumes have become the junk mail of the nineties.** With the proliferation of the personal computer and the fax machine, it has become easier than ever to generate a customized resume (to increase micromarketing effectiveness) and easier still to fax the resume to the potential employer. As a result, more people reply to more ads than ever before and with less time spent by job searchers in determining whether the job opening is potentially a good "fit."

Where to Find the Candidates

Believe it or not, the most difficult task for employers who want to fill positions is to determine where they are most likely to find suitable candidates. It is easy to boast about the response of an ad but the best response is the one that concludes with a new hire. The size of the response is irrelevant. Whether it is 1 or 401 responses, that effort is for naught if none of the people who surface is appropriate for the open position. The truth is that basic job requirements are becoming more demanding at the same time our general population has problems with science, technology, mathematical skills, communications skills, and literacy.

From an Applicant's Viewpoint

Applicants have a harder than ever job to find appropriate jobs. Consider the following circumstances.

Where to Look?

The decision of where to apply is difficult, and the competition wherever you do go is heavy. Once the path is taken, the obstacles are huge. The time required to look is increasing because the access has grown. Think about it. In the not too distant past, technology was limited, mobility was less, and sources of information were fewer and harder to access than now. The positive side was that you could focus on what was close and important. Your choices were limited and therefore you had a clearer idea of what was most relevant to pursue. Friends, relatives, and neighbors all helped to identify opportunities in a narrow band of opportunity.

Now contemplate the current situation. Even when you get a lead and prepare to respond, the obstacles take other challenging forms. Each advertisement or job opening elicits hundreds of resumes and letters, putting a burden on the person screening. If your resume and letter hits a responsive chord, or if you are able to lock in a contact to get you in the door, you finally get to speak to the organization.

So Many People, So Little Opportunity

Many people out there are searching for a position. Many more people are looking for jobs than there are jobs available. Some say that anyone who wants a job always gets one, and that is probably true. But all that means is that there are plenty of jobs at the low wage end, but they quickly evaporate as one goes looking up the scale. A look at those 400 resumes received in response to an ad would show that many are not even close to the job requirements.

The Proliferation of Resumes

It is so hard to be considered for any job because, once an ad is placed, the organization is flooded with resumes. The problem is getting your resume noticed and picked from all the others received. **Your resume must rise to the top on the wave of paper submitted.** It is just not enough to assume your resume sparkles because of your specific relevant experience. It needs to have visibility and be separated from all the others. This presumes a timely arrival, a visually attractive document, and dependence on the person screening the resume to be able to identify that particularly relevant experience.

Wild Goose Chases

There seem to be more false starts in the hiring process than at any time in recent memory. A false start is the all-out effort to hire a person for a specific position (or what seems to be a specific position) only to find that the effort is aborted for a variety of reasons. *"The position is put on hold." "We are rethinking our strategy ... reorganizing ... eliminating the department ... merging into a group function."* This disheartening news can be presented anytime during the search and even midway through the hire offer. *The Wall Street Journal* carried a front page story of the public servant from Boston who accepted a job with a major Wall Street firm. The day he was to start the job, after relocating from Boston, he read *The Wall Street Journal* on the way to work and the page one headline disclosed that his unit was about to be shut down. He was forced to go back into the job market.

The Person Interviewing You Is
So Young and/or Inexperienced

The older you get, the younger the interviewer looks. That is not just the comment of an older job applicant. It is often true because in many organizations there are a variety of misperceptions about the skills required to be an effective interviewer. There continues to be a lack of concern for the training and development of the individuals in the organization entrusted with the most important task of identifying suitable candidates for the organization.

Where and How to Find the Jobs

If one of the greatest challenges for employers is to find suitable candidates, *the biggest frustration for job seekers is to find the employers who are looking for candidates.* In spite of downsizing, the United States continues to have a vibrant and resilient economy. Unfortunately, part of that environment includes different organizations going through certain stages of their life cycles at the same time. While new industries are going through periods of explosive growth, others are in their maturity stage, and still others are in a period of decline. The not-for-profit and governmental sectors have their life cycles too. The point to keep in mind is that this vibrant economy is constantly making jobs available at the same time jobs are being eliminated. The United States Chamber of Commerce and Industry is not alone in saying it does not know how many businesses are in operation at any one point in time, because at the precise moment some businesses are opening their doors for the first time, other are closing theirs. The Chamber estimates that at the present time there are approximately 11 million businesses operating in the United States. Think of that number for a moment: that is 11 million businesses in the private sector. That number does not include the various agencies of the government and the numerous organizations in the not-for-profit sector.

The challenge for the job seeker is to determine which of those 11 million businesses are the most appropriate.

Where You Are Coming from

Depending on how you got the lead for the interview, your chances of landing the job depend on many different factors. Using recruiters, classified ads, and even the information highway (electronic bulletin boards) has both advantages and disadvantages for the applicant.

My book, *How to Find a Job in 90 Days or Less,* describes a three-step process that commences with a personal assessment. Once that is done the next step is to determine a marketing plan. The marketing plan considers your knowledge, skills, abilities, experiences, likes, and dislikes, and then puts them aside while taking the time to determine the organizations that will be most appropriate and desirable for you to consider further as opportunities for employment. The last step in the process is to implement an action plan to link your desires and wishes to your skills and abilities. These steps lead you to the interview.

Employer's Choices in Candidate Search	Advantages to Applicant	Disadvantages to Applicant
Job postings (internal)	Limited pool of applicants	Unknown to applicant if not already employed there
Recruiters, agencies	They (may) have job orders and openings	Fees paid by employer Longer time frame Additional screening levels
Electronic bulletin boards	Limited pool of applicants	Limited access Limited employers
Advertisements	One-stop source	Too large response Too many candidates
Professional associations	Member of a high-caliber talent pool	Limited to certain groups Unable to control the timely dissemination of information for the vacancy
Schools	Known quality	Limited access Entry level only
Public (governmental) agencies	No fee Indication of good faith efforts to adhere to EEO guideline	Little or no screening of candidates more likely than not
Billboards	High visibility	High visibility
Radio/TV	Wide reach Limited pool	Without volume, high cost
Referrals	Get inside track	Friendship may be on line if job does not work out

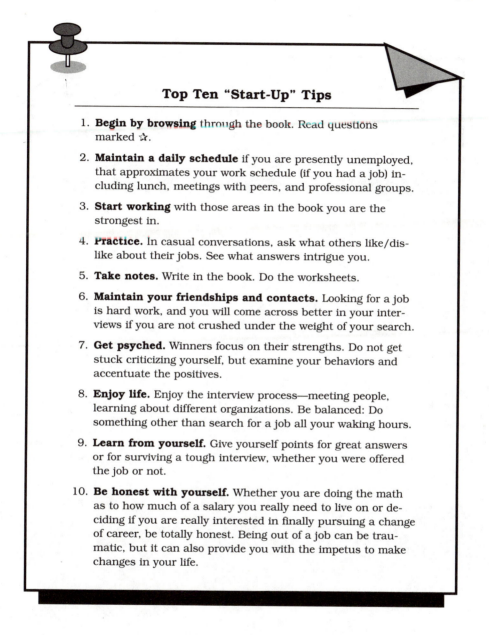

Top Ten "Start-Up" Tips

1. **Begin by browsing** through the book. Read questions marked ☆.

2. **Maintain a daily schedule** if you are presently unemployed, that approximates your work schedule (if you had a job) including lunch, meetings with peers, and professional groups.

3. **Start working** with those areas in the book you are the strongest in.

4. **Practice.** In casual conversations, ask what others like/dislike about their jobs. See what answers intrigue you.

5. **Take notes.** Write in the book. Do the worksheets.

6. **Maintain your friendships and contacts.** Looking for a job is hard work, and you will come across better in your interviews if you are not crushed under the weight of your search.

7. **Get psyched.** Winners focus on their strengths. Do not get stuck criticizing yourself, but examine your behaviors and accentuate the positives.

8. **Enjoy life.** Enjoy the interview process—meeting people, learning about different organizations. Be balanced: Do something other than search for a job all your waking hours.

9. **Learn from yourself.** Give yourself points for great answers or for surviving a tough interview, whether you were offered the job or not.

10. **Be honest with yourself.** Whether you are doing the math as to how much of a salary you really need to live on or deciding if you are really interested in finally pursuing a change of career, be totally honest. Being out of a job can be traumatic, but it can also provide you with the impetus to make changes in your life.

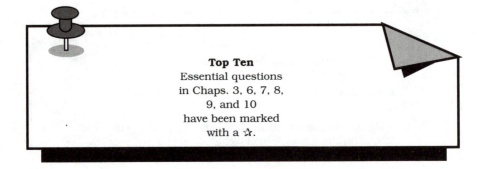

Top Ten
Essential questions
in Chaps. 3, 6, 7, 8,
9, and 10
have been marked
with a ☆.

2

Tips on Communication

Talking Is Not Communicating

An interview is a conversation with a specific purpose. Both parties to the interview want something from the process. So the goal of the interview for both parties is to feel that they have achieved their goals. The greater the area of common goals met, the greater the probability of a job offer.

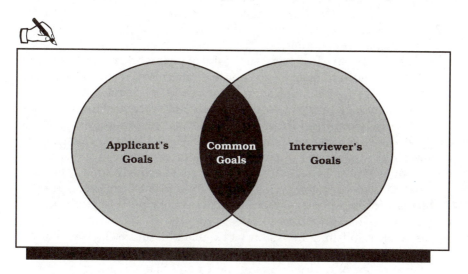

What are the interviewer's goals? Ostensibly, to fill the position. However, there are excellent, good, and poor interviewers out there, and **the interviewer's apparent agenda at an interview may differ widely from the hidden agenda:**

❑ Is this a courtesy interview?

❑ Is the position all but filled internally and the organization is just going through the motions of a search?

❑ What else is going on politically in the organization?

❑ What kind of day is the interviewer having?

❑ What is the interviewer's next appointment?

❑ Is the interview running late?

Importance of Knowledge Workers Who Are Excellent Communicators

Why should the interview count for so much when speaking is *not* the most important requirement for the job? Job seekers are frequently frustrated and feel hampered because they lack confidence in their oral communication ability. Additionally, the person trying to find a job may resent the interview process because it represents a real or perceived hurdle that serves as an impediment to job offers. (*"I'm looking for a job, not to have meetings. Why can't they judge me by reviewing my paperwork and giving me a written test? The position I seek does not require interviewing skills anyway."*)

This is a source of real frustration about the interview process. Applicants may be unable to communicate their work experience effectively even though they may have been very successful at their work, possibly even an expert in the field. The question may be legitimate: What is the relevance of the interview if oral communication is not a major job requirement?

While many jobs may not require constant interaction with other employees, **it is becoming increasingly important to communicate effectively at work regardless of your position.** Technology and change—the hallmarks of our current everyday environment—make it increasingly important always to be ready to communicate effectively. In fact, the reason that most people are not able to retain current positions is due to problems with interpersonal relationships on the job. Failure to communicate can be a real drawback to career progress.

The gurus publishing books on work-related issues today seem to all agree that we are living in a postindustrial age. Approximately only 20 percent of all employed workers in the United States work in manufacturing companies. The vast majority work in the service sector, and a smaller and smaller portion are in agriculture. These numbers have had no significant change in quite a few years. So what is portrayed now as a sudden change has been a reality for a while.

The knowledge worker, on the other hand, is a concept that is very recent. Even though traditionally employers have usually frowned on the notion of the indispensability of the worker (the goal was to seek the opposite), now there is a growing realization that *the most desired workers are those who bring their knowledge with them to the job.* What the employer imparts and employees absorb is a variety of mental concepts to build a personal database in their heads that grows increasingly valuable to the employer. In fact, even in manufacturing, it is begrudgingly accepted that even the assembly line worker (the most obvious object of the attempt to make every worker truly dispensable) is a "knowledge" worker. Employers are conceding the importance of the skill base that workers build as they grow with the organization. In the most manual and labor-intensive of jobs, the incumbents performing the jobs are appreciated more than ever. As a case in point, the automobile industry is very concerned at the increasing average age of the automobile worker—exacerbated by the massive layoffs of the 1970s, 1980s and, bizarre as it seems, still in the 1990s. In particular, Chrysler is worried about the staff levels it is now anticipating it will need as more and more of its assembly line workers approach retirement.

If the knowledge worker is becoming increasingly important, how does an employer determine which applicant has the experience (or potential) to be an effective worker in an environment where knowledge is so important? So much of what is perceived to be "job-related knowledge" is intangible that, even if it could be determined with a written test, the time and expense used to develop the test is not something that is seen as an alternative by many employers. The most common alternative and the most practical choice is the "hands-on," personal interview, in which candidates are sized up, their work and education experience is evaluated, and their potential is assessed.

The Interview Process

Invitations to interview are the keys to the job search process. The more opportunities you get to be considered for available openings, the more likely you will have a job search that leads to one or more desirable offers. The more that you interview, the better you get.

In an interview, the first step is to determine that both the interviewer and interviewee agree on the **purpose of the meeting.** Are you looking to fill a specific position? Is this position open? Do you meet the requirements of the position? Given the job description, are you interested in the position as it currently exists?

Who is the "buyer" and who is the "seller" in the interview? What is more important to you, do you hear the interviewer's message, and does the interviewer hear yours? What exactly do you want to get out of this interview? What do you want to "give" the interviewer?

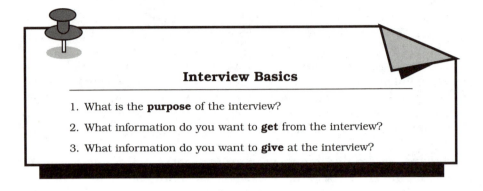

Interview Basics

1. What is the **purpose** of the interview?
2. What information do you want to **get** from the interview?
3. What information do you want to **give** at the interview?

Hearing Versus Listening

Hearing involves your ears while listening also involves your mind. Active listening involves your entire self. In the classroom, you learn how to read, write, and speak, but how much time have you spent learning how to listen? In normal conversations, with no agendas, many times we are too often thinking of the next point we want to make or how we can break into the conversation rather than to what is actually being said. How often, when you are introduced to a stranger by a friend, are you so concerned with having *your name* pronounced correctly that you end up walking away from the introduction not knowing the other person's name? That, unfortunately, is human nature. How much more difficult can an interview be when you may feel that so much is on the line?

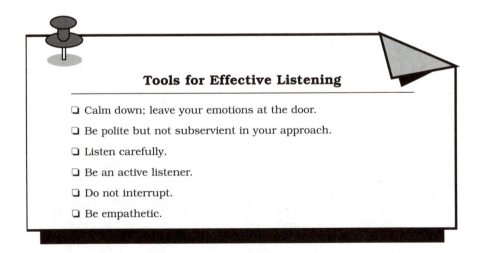

Tools for Effective Listening

❑ Calm down; leave your emotions at the door.

❑ Be polite but not subservient in your approach.

❑ Listen carefully.

❑ Be an active listener.

❑ Do not interrupt.

❑ Be empathetic.

The first step in becoming a better listener—an active listener—is to start right now. In all your conversations—with family, friends, "small talk" with strangers—slow it down and start listening.

Put your emotions on hold.   Quit worrying about coming up with snappy answers; it is perfectly fine to hesitate a moment to "gather your thoughts" before answering. These pauses can be easily read as a sign of respect, an acknowledgment of the importance of the question. Take a quiet, calming breath. Unclench those hands and sit comfortably in the chair. Train your focus on the person who is speaking. Is he or she speaking fast or slowly? How much eye contact is there? **Differences in style can create tension, but accepting differences can help you concentrate, which can lead to better understanding.**

Do not label the speaker.   Do not become so impressed that the interviewer is "giver of jobs" that this becomes a block to effective listening. Listen to everyone without prejudice as to the source of the information. What you do with the information can be decided later when you can "consider the source." Do not put up barriers to your listening.

Listen actively.   Do not be afraid to ask questions to further the information being given. Show the speaker that you are listening by offering eye contact. Make slight gestures of affirmation (a smile, nodding the head, comments) to show that your attention is with the speaker. If you do not understand a point, ask that it be explained further or restate it, "… *in other words, you are looking for …*"

Do not assume anything.   Think of the game show "Jeopardy." How many times have you seen the contestant ring the buzzer with a response before the "answer" has been given in its entirety—only to be wrong? Do not jump to conclusions. Gather all the information available before offering a comment or solution. **Let the interviewer ask the question completely.** Jumping in too early can make speakers feel that they are doing a poor job of communicating because you just cannot wait to go where they are not heading!

Put yourself in the other person's shoes.   What is the speaker looking for? What are the other person's needs? **You can try to sway other persons' opinions or obtain influence only after you understand them.** Look for issues or unsatisfied needs as "buttons" to push. *You are offering yourself as a solution to someone else's problems;* you must listen closely to determine specifically what those problems are and how you can uniquely solve them.

The Actual Face-to-Face Meeting

After all your preparation, letter writing, resume mailings, and telephone follow-ups, the day of the interview has arrived. Call to confirm the place and time. Plan your route and transportation, and allow ample time to arrive a few minutes early for your interview. **The interview process starts the moment of your arrival.**

Once you enter the building, be alert and listen to what is going on around you. All your senses should be operating to evaluate this organization as one in which you may choose to spend most of your waking hours for years to come. Consider the overall appearance of the offices and the attitudes of employees that you encounter.

If you can think of the interview as similar to a "first date," then the meeting place should be evaluated in terms of the importance the employer places on these dates. Instead of parents meeting you at the door and giving you the once-over, every employee you come in contact with (particularly in the reception area) could give feedback about you to the decision makers. This is a two-way street: you are also evaluating the organization through the actions and attitudes of the employees you meet.

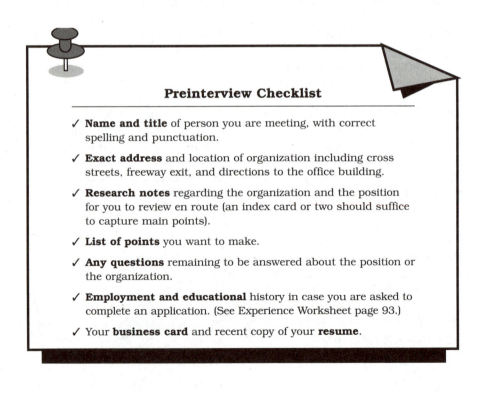

Preinterview Checklist

✓ **Name and title** of person you are meeting, with correct spelling and punctuation.

✓ **Exact address** and location of organization including cross streets, freeway exit, and directions to the office building.

✓ **Research notes** regarding the organization and the position for you to review en route (an index card or two should suffice to capture main points).

✓ **List of points** you want to make.

✓ **Any questions** remaining to be answered about the position or the organization.

✓ **Employment and educational** history in case you are asked to complete an application. (See Experience Worksheet page 93.)

✓ Your **business card** and recent copy of your **resume**.

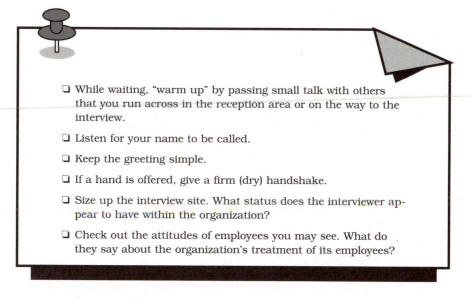

❏ While waiting, "warm up" by passing small talk with others that you run across in the reception area or on the way to the interview.

❏ Listen for your name to be called.

❏ Keep the greeting simple.

❏ If a hand is offered, give a firm (dry) handshake.

❏ Size up the interview site. What status does the interviewer appear to have within the organization?

❏ Check out the attitudes of employees you may see. What do they say about the organization's treatment of its employees?

You Meet Your "Date"

Even though some may not consider the interviewer's greeting and your response important, they are missing an important part of the meeting. A person is evaluated after the meeting based on the rapport established at the meeting, in addition to the responses provided throughout the meeting. **Applicants who take seriously every message they send during and throughout any interaction are much more in control of their messages and are more effective throughout the process.**

Since you have taken time to consider how you present (or sell) yourself, from packaging (your attire and resume) to content (the research and analysis that preceded the interview), it is only fair for you to evaluate

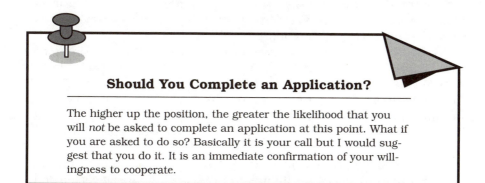

Should You Complete an Application?

The higher up the position, the greater the likelihood that you will *not* be asked to complete an application at this point. What if you are asked to do so? Basically it is your call but I would suggest that you do it. It is an immediate confirmation of your willingness to cooperate.

how the organization presents itself. The interview location is the "sales office." Are they making any effort to "sell" themselves to you as a prospective employer?

The Interview Site

The interview site is a great opportunity for you to be a communication sponge. Consider what messages the meeting place says about the importance the organizational places on the person you are meeting and the importance the organization places on the meeting itself.

Consider the meeting room and everything about it. What floor is it on? What other organizational units are located on the same floor? (Check out the floor directory or the one in the lobby.) Then look around the room. Is there a door (for privacy)? Does the room have windows? A view? The furniture, fixtures, and artwork or other items displayed on the walls set a tone. Does the room have time-sensitive material displayed? For example, it's November and there are notices for the company picnic, or some of the "employee of the month" plaques are missing for several past months. What do these notices reveal about the organization and its occupants? Do the walls boast of motivation posters? Soak it all up. You need to learn as much as you can about what the organization wants to project as an image. You need to confirm in your own mind a consistency or inconsistency in their messages.

The Meeting Itself

This is why you are there. Be alert to all your surroundings and to the presentation of your interviewer. If you have received a letter with the interviewer's name and title in confirmation of your interview, be certain to use the person's name—Mr., Mrs., or Ms. So-and-so. Don't be too informal and use first names unless invited to do so and be willing to reciprocate. If you do not have this person's name and title, ask for a business card. Use the person's name as soon as possible. Doing so helps you to remember it and to establish rapport.

Psychologists say that, when we meet another person, we determine whether we like them or not within 25 seconds after the meeting starts. Keep that finding in mind during your interviewing process and do not forget that the sword cuts two ways: You are meeting the other person for the first time as well. "Judge not lest you be judged." It is to be hoped that both of you separately determine your initial conclusions and then spend the rest of the meeting trying to determine the accuracy of them. Do not in any event tune out of the meeting because of your first impression. Always be professional and see it through to its conclusion. The person you are meeting with probably feels obligated to do the same.

The Concept of Time

Pay careful notice to the organization's use of time before, during, and even after the meeting takes place. These displays, while sometimes subtle, are indicators of the organization's view of time. The use or abuse of time may be conditioned by the nature of the organization's business. Ultimately, the view of time is expressed by the persons who set the tone for the organization.

Let me give an example. If 15 minutes and then a half-hour pass before your scheduled meeting occurs, the delay might be just an unusual occurrence or it might be the organization's approach to time. What should you do? Is anyone aware of the fact that your appointed time has come and gone? Does the receptionist think this is no big deal? Is the person you are to meet with even in the building? If you are appalled by the disregard for your presence and that is intolerable to you, then you need to vote with your feet to remove yourself from the premises. No matter how desperate you are, **if tardiness or disregard for time is a deal-breaking item for you, be ready to recognize it when it occurs and deal with it immediately.**

More subtle time pieces and characteristics have to do with what takes place during the meeting. Does the interviewer get interrupted for calls? Was he or she asked to step out of the room? Was a closed door ignored? Was the door even closed? Try to listen without snooping and see whether the interviewer provides additional data so that you can determine for yourself what is going on organizationally. (Of course, never repeat the information gleaned at any interview.)

Farewell (See You Soon?)

The last part of the interview, after all the small and big talk, is the most important part. Where are matters left? Do they want more information from you? Do you want to follow up with them? What is the next step? When will they make their decision? Should you be meeting other people? Is another interview to be scheduled? For details on this portion of the progress, see Chap. 14, "Summing Up: Now What?"

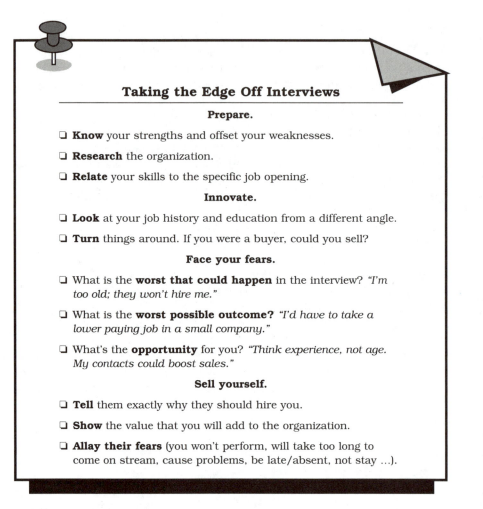

Taking the Edge Off Interviews

Prepare.

❏ **Know** your strengths and offset your weaknesses.

❏ **Research** the organization.

❏ **Relate** your skills to the specific job opening.

Innovate.

❏ **Look** at your job history and education from a different angle.

❏ **Turn** things around. If you were a buyer, could you sell?

Face your fears.

❏ What is the **worst that could happen** in the interview? *"I'm too old; they won't hire me."*

❏ What is the **worst possible outcome?** *"I'd have to take a lower paying job in a small company."*

❏ What's the **opportunity** for you? *"Think experience, not age. My contacts could boost sales."*

Sell yourself.

❏ **Tell** them exactly why they should hire you.

❏ **Show** the value that you will add to the organization.

❏ **Allay their fears** (you won't perform, will take too long to come on stream, cause problems, be late/absent, not stay ...).

3

Are You an Open Book?

How Much Do I Need to Disclose?

As competition continues to pose an increasing challenge to each job applicant, successful persons are those who are best able to get an edge over everybody else. The persons with the best networks, marketing letters, and resumes are able to get a foot into the door.

Once inside, though, those who are best able to deal with the interview and all its nuances are successful in getting a job offer. Listening, nonverbal communication, awareness, and perception are all invaluable elements in the communication process. Another important element in the communication process is disclosure.

What Do I Have to Share with Interviewers?

Disclosure is the sharing of information. It is up to you to decide how much information you wish to share, the extent you choose to share it, and how you want to share it. You may disclose something verbally (in written or oral format) or nonverbally (remember the old poker face?). Anytime a question is asked—whatever the setting—in providing the answer, you determine consciously or unconsciously how much information you choose to share with the person raising the question. Share too much too quickly, and others may back away because you are sharing more than they want to hear. Share too little or too slowly, and others may feel that you are being unfriendly. They may consider withdrawing from the encounter because their attempts at conversation are not being answered sufficiently.

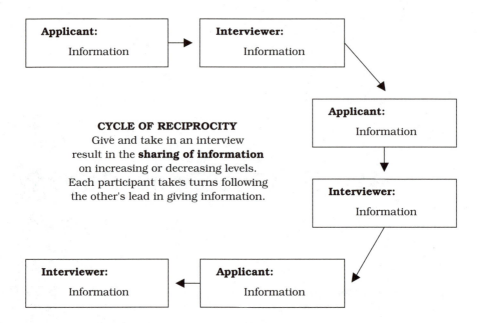

Reciprocity

The objective of any conversation (which is what an interview is, don't forget) is to exchange information at a level that is appropriate and acceptable to both parties. Just as in social settings, in an interview there is an unstated-stated agreement between the two participants that, if sufficient and applicable information is supplied by the applicant, the interviewer reciprocates by letting the recruitment and selection process continue and ultimately by making the job offer.

Interviewing and Dating

Again, think of the recruitment process as a courtship and the interview as a date. Both the interviewer and the job applicant are jockeying for position to determine whether or not the relationship should go further. For example, sharing a variety of facts on a first date may scare the other person away immediately. Or, during a casual discussion between two strangers who talk on a plane, what is required is to **gradually share** information on an equivalent basis. One person might say something about where they work and the other does the same. If one does and the other does not, the informal rules say that there is an inequity and an ineffective communication exchange results. The ultimate result is seen in behavior (i.e., no chance to get another date with the same person or an additional interview with the same organization). There is no mystique.

So too in the recruitment and selection process. As in dating, if too much is disclosed too quickly, the person receiving the information is overwhelmed and becomes concerned with what he/she has just learned. The interviewer is interested in absorbing only as much information as is required for each step in the process.

❏ *Don't be too aggressive:* "No one tells me what to do until they earn my respect."

❏ *Don't get too detailed:* A ten-minute explanation of your trip in response to, "How was the trip here?"

❏ *Don't get too personal:* "I was abused as a child, just divorced by my third spouse, and now have ten kids."

Understand and appreciate this fact so that you disclose neither too much nor too little information at any given point in the interview. For example, the applicant goes into elaborate and technical detail about the intricacies of a position, boring the interviewer to the extent that the interviewer dismisses the applicant as verbose. If, on the other hand, the applicant can get through the first "gatekeeper," the line manager would welcome the display of technical proficiency and state-of-the-art knowledge. **If you disclose information before the interviewer needs its, you run the real risk that the interviewer:**

❏ **Either knows everything about the applicant too early** (such as when the interviewer is still in the recruitment phase of the process). So there is no reason to continue the interviewing process (during the selection phase). When this happens, the only thing left to do will be to decide whether to hire or not.

❏ **Or is overwhelmed** and does not like that so much has been disclosed. Here the real risk is that the applicant shares with the Personnel/Human Resource interviewer information best saved for the interview with the line manager.

It is better simply to create the perception that you are astute in the role of a professional and understand the nuances of interviewing, including the principle of disclosure. In other words, don't go too fast too early in the process.

A Word About Jargon

The use of technical, "insider" language is a form of disclosure. By using it, you are sharing a certain level of technical knowledge that would not have been known if you had chosen not to share it. If you use technical jargon in the right environment, you are considered articulate, astute, and in possession of state-of-the-art knowledge. In the wrong situation you will be taken as pompous, pretentious, and a bore.

If you want to use jargon, be sure you are current and up-to-date. For example, there is nothing more embarrassing in the Personnel/Human Resource profession than to hear applicants mention (or, worse, include on the resume) that they are members of ASPA (the American Society of Personnel Administrators) when the organization changed its name almost ten years ago to SHRM (Society for Human Resource Management).

Utilize Disclosure Effectively

Job applicants who are sensitive to the principle of disclosure are more effective during the interview process. They are able to better control the flow of the information they are sharing and are more sensitive to what they are saying consistently throughout the process.

With regard to illegal questions, even though you should not be asked certain questions, there is nothing to prevent you from offering information if you feel it will enhance your candidacy.

> *Since I have no children and plan not to for the near future, I am totally open to any and all travel plans required of the position, including relocation.*
>
> *Since I visited with relatives in Italy during my college vacations and was employed there for a few years after graduation, I have a profound and practical insight on the Italian economy that can prove to be invaluable in the travel business.*

Soldiers are trained, if captured by the enemy, to only provide name, rank, and serial number. They are told that there is more likelihood of survival if they retain information. Once the enemy gets captives to open up and share everything they know, the need to keep them alive drops dramatically.

So too during the interview process, **you can keep your candidacy "alive" by not baring your soul at the first opportunity.** Consider the **gradual dissemination of information** at the pace sought by the interviewer. You are then nonverbally communicating that you understand the dynamics of the process and can share on a "need to know basis," providing only the information at the appropriate level of detail when it is sought.

Disclosure can work for you if you understand that withholding and disseminating of information give you a form of control during the interviewing process. **Share information if it is to be of assistance to you. Withhold information if it is to be considered detrimental. Under no circumstances lie.**

⭐ **3.1   What were your positions, rates of pay, dates of employment, name and title of supervisors for the past ____ year(s)?   (data)**

The information requested here is data that you should have available at a moment's notice because every organization requires that you provide it. Usually this is all obtained uniformly with an employment application. Regardless of the job level, if you are asked to complete an application, do so. You may try writing in the experience section "see resume" if you prefer, and the burden is on the HR/Personnel staff to notice what you have done. The fact is that your resume does not provide the same information requested in applications. The question is whether the Personnel Department in the organization reviews the form while you are there and asks you for additional information. The most obvious details missing from most resumes (and that is as it should be according to the principle of disclosure) are rate of pay and the reasons for leaving other positions.

If you prefer, you may also consider asking if you may complete the application at home. Whatever you do, do not get into an argument with a clerk who may report back to the boss that you refused to complete an employment application. More often than not, your candidacy ends right there.

Be consistent in the details on the application and on the resume. Particular areas are dates and job titles. Be aware of salary information you choose to provide on the application because the question may come up during the interview, and you must provide a consistent answer. Otherwise, you are opening yourself up for additional questions, and your credibility may ultimately be questioned because of a discrepancy.

3.2   How did you get your last job?

Was it planned or happenstance? Planning it demonstrates to the interviewer your sense of mission and purpose, and it indicates that you are a person who plans and takes action. If you stumbled upon your last job, the answer is just not as strong regardless of the circumstances. You need to prepare a polished answer that presents the situation in the best light possible.

⭐ **3.3 What is the reason you left/are planning to leave _____ organization?**

Be careful that your motivation is not totally selfish. Do not whine that they would not promote you (or give you an increase, a corner office, a higher commission schedule). Instead take a broader view.

❑ *"They weren't keeping up with the competition."*
❑ *"They were unwilling to provide the necessary resources to meet their five-year plan."*

3.4 How did you hear about this position?

This answer demonstrates the quality of your sources of information. If your neighbor happens to be the chairperson and CEO of the organization you are meeting with (or any other employee, for that matter), do not hesitate to mention that he or she told you about the opening. As a rule, internal introductions work as effectively as anything that is warmer than a cold sales call. On the other hand, do not portray the referral as something it isn't. If you have no connection directly to the employee (it is through your parent, for example), be honest about it. Once the person is mentioned, the interviewer is very likely to pursue the comment to determine the nature of the relationship. It is better to hear it from you now than from the employee later.

3.5 Have you received any other job offers? What other organizations or positions are you considering?

Employers like job applicants who are actively sought by others. Once you admit that you have other offers pending, you need to be careful not to disclose the wrong information. Some employers have disdain and outright scorn for competitors and others in the marketplace. To admit that you have another offer makes you appear attractive to your interviewer. The more you disclose after that, the more you risk taking the glow off the statement. For example, a major money center commercial bank looks with disdain at an offer from a smaller savings bank. To an investment bank recruiter, it may seem odd for a graduating MBA to consider a position in manufacturing (gasp!) or retailing (even worse!).

3.6 What do you do with your spare time?

This is not being asked idly, as part of small talk in the opening of the interview. The interviewer is looking for insights into your personality. Be consistent with your resume and application information furnished previously.

There are two points not to be missed: First, **your response could "define" you** to the interviewer. What you choose to do may say a lot about who you are. Are you active (*"avid runner"*) or passive (*"watch sports"*), a loner (*"write poetry"*) or a joiner (*"volunteer in a local soup kitchen"*). Second, the person interviewing you may have a **particular interest in what you say.** Be prepared to discuss the subject in more detail if called on to do so. If you do not want to open this door, omit the information from your resume and application forms.

3.7 What are you doing now to attain a goal you have set for yourself?

Start the answer with a definition of the goal. It may be job-related (*"... to move to the next position within one year"*) or not (*"... to return to school and get the degree I have postponed for so long"*). Once the goal has been defined, be ready to demonstrate how you have started to go about it. If you can include a timetable, do so. It demonstrates all the more forcefully that your planning includes a time element.

☆ 3.8 What is your current salary?

Tread carefully. There are three ways to consider this question.

1. *Did you fill out an application?* If so, they already have the information, so be consistent.

2. *Do you know the salary range for the open position (from ad, recruiter, insider information)? Answer with a range, if possible* ("Mid-thirties before commissions"). **Negotiate salary when the job is offered, not before.**

3. *You have no idea what the open position pays.* If you come in too low, you may be taken up at a "cheap" price; too high, and you have priced yourself out of the job. Couch your response by giving an accurate amount, and if you feel it is too low, add, *"That is base salary exclusive of perks and benefits that are quite generous and should be considered a part of a total compensation package."*

Remember Some employers insist that, when you are hired, you provide a copy of your most recent pay stub to confirm the accuracy of your stated salary.

If the question is phrased *"What do you feel this position should pay?"* it is easier to deal with, but it is still stressful because salary is always a delicate topic. In this instance, you may defer if you do not have a reasonable understanding of the position's responsibilities and scope. You may also ask for assistance from the interviewer. Ask if there are similar positions in the organizations (in the same salary range). Once the interviewer shares some information (unless the position is truly unique, which is very rare), you may project for this position not so much a salary, but a salary range (if in fact the interviewer does not share any data with you).

3.9 Have you ever been denied a salary increase?

A "yes" portrays you as a person with a problem, regardless of the situation in the organization. Being denied a salary increase is different from just not getting a salary increase. For an affirmative answer, you needed at least once in your life to go to your boss and be denied a salary increase when one was requested. This does not include times when one was expected. Remember the times when you might have asked for one and eventually got it. I would not even recommend you consider a situation that warrants a "yes" answer. **An unqualified negative reply is always the best and the strongest answer.**

3.10 Were you ever asked to take a pay cut? Describe the circumstances.

Although taking a pay cut is different from being denied a pay increase, an explanation is required if you have ever agreed to one. With a pay cut the circumstances may have required your acceptance for the good of the organization. If an equity offer was included (as the airlines have recently been doing), then you are showing yourself to be a person with a reasonable yet long-term view that also expresses faith in (and loyalty to) the organization.

☆ 3.11 Have you ever been asked to resign?

Determine in advance how to handle this question if the answer is affirmative. Admit it to the interviewer, disclosing the circumstances as briefly and objectively as possible. When faced with an ultimatum from an employer, the scar is usually deep and longlasting (if not permanent). Present an objective spin and demonstrate a firm, confident conviction that you benefited from the experience.

I was asked to resign at XYZ corporation because there was a major down-scale of activities and I was given the choice of taking a position of less responsibility or leaving. If I had taken the lower-level position, there still would have been no guarantee that that job would have any more security. If I had stayed, the severance package may have been less or none at all. So I left. It really worked out well, though, because I quickly found a position at DEF Industries with a 20 percent increase in compensation. As you know, XYZ on the other hand shortly thereafter went out of existence entirely and 200 employees were out of work with only unemployment benefits at their disposal.

As with any other factual responses, be certain that your version is corroborated by your former employer(s).

☆ 3.12 *Were you ever fired? Describe the circumstances.*

Eighty percent of all terminations are the result of work relationship problems, according to a recent survey of outplaced employee clients by a major outplacement firm. Remember this when considering your response to this question. If you were the object of a mutual agreement resignation (and you took the option of resigning), you should think at least twice before responding in the affirmative. If it happened, admit it and end with a comment to the effect that, *"I certainly learned from this experience."*

There are many reasons why a person gets fired, including:

❑ *Poor interpersonal relationships with your boss, colleagues, subordinates, your boss's boss.* As mentioned, displaced employees frequently identify poor interpersonal relations as the primary cause for their termination of employment. If this is the reason you left your job, do not share that fact with the interviewer. Even if you firmly believe that relationships with only one type of person will make you an effective employee, I would not disclose it.

Be mindful of the fact that dismissals are usually complex affairs. Even if you feel that your relationship with your boss was the reason you were fired, think about what you are about to disclose and consider the ramifications seriously. If you admit you had a tough time getting along with your boss (who, by the way, may have been the worst boss in the world), that is one thing. If in addition you admit to being fired (as opposed to walking out), then you are admitting to two major facts of disclosure: failure to "get along" and being fired.

What if you were given the option to resign? Then you can say you resigned. How much more you wish to share is up to you. But if you sound like a problem employee, you will not get the job.

❏ *Incompetence.* This is complicated. If you were fired because you could not do the job, how does it sound to the person who is interviewing you? The first question to follow may be, *"Why was this not detected during their selection process?"* Before considering admitting to this one, determine whether the job they are considering you for is similar (or, worse, identical) in responsibility to the one you were just fired from. The only out is along the lines of *"... the responsibilities of the position were significantly altered between the time I was hired and the time I started."* You must then be prepared to give the circumstances surrounding the situation to briefly describe the events that altered the scope of the position—a restructuring, new technology, the hire or departure of a player who was key to the position you were to occupy, etc.

❏ *Lack of work or job elimination.* This is a common occurrence today and is easily accepted by potential employers. Keep in mind the outplacement survey that concluded 80 percent of all terminations are the result of work relationship problems. Usually employers feel that they and other organizations try to save their best employees regardless of the situation. If you lost your job because the position was eliminated, be careful not to use the word "fired" if you can avoid it. *"Terminated," "laid off," "given a [severance] package"* are all euphemisms that set a tone that *the loss of your job was due not to your performance* but to circumstances beyond your control.

❏ *Illegal reasons including past worker's compensation claims, discrimination based on prohibited categories, and sexual harassment.* A word of advice: *Never, never, never mention to a future employer that you lost your most recent job because you were a victim either of discrimination* (based on either sex, race, creed, color, national origin, age, marital status, Vietnam era veteran, or disability) *or of sexual harassment* (making the granting of unwanted sexual attention a term or condition of your continued employment, or worse, if you were the person accused of the harassment). If you do disclose any such thing, the interviewer may dismiss you as a candidate. No one will admit that the reason for losing interest in your candidacy is your candor; to do so would put the interviewer and the organization at risk.

3.13 Describe a few situations where your work was criticized.

This is a probing question raised by an experienced (and/or well trained) interviewer. The answer you provide offers the interviewer an opportunity to consider:

❏ Your *ability to communicate effectively* with a situation that is extremely personal yet at the same time totally professional.

❏ Your *tolerance* for criticism.

❏ The *scope* of your activities and projects.

❏ The level of your *participation* in those activities and projects.

❏ The *environment* in which you have been working.

All this from this one nonhostile, totally open-ended question!

Ideally, consider describing situations that show your work was criticized, but portray them as being borne out by the situation itself. Also consider very "gray" situations because usually your judgment is not being assessed as wrong and the interviewer can recognize that, in some instances, a risk has to be taken. Refer to your Experience Worksheet (page 93) and Critical Incidents Worksheet (page 94) to refresh your memory.

Here are some sample responses:

> *I recall when New York City was threatened by a hurricane and I made it a point to get in early because in Human Resource I thought there would be a lot of people-related issues to deal with. As luck would have it, the hurricane was to pass the city at approximately 10:00 A.M.—a time when everybody was scheduled to be already in. Therefore, those at work would not be challenged by the hurricane unless the building itself was threatened. In an effort to thank all the employees who had bothered to show up for work (and keep them at work—the inclement weather could wreak all sorts of havoc with people on the street). I determined and recommended to management that all employees at work be invited to use the cafeteria for lunch that day at no cost and determined that this would cost the company approximately $600. Management was concerned that I had lost my mind and wondered about the soundness of the proposal. It was no big deal, but I accepted their decision and tried to fathom why the strong negative response. I was never able to.*

> *We were under a great deal of pressure to meet the deadline on a project to install payroll software, and it needed to be done by the end of the year. In a task force meeting that no one wanted to attend, the technical people would not offer a target date for the completion of the installation. Since they wouldn't, I did. After the meeting I learned that they complained to my boss and were incensed that I was so "heavy-handed." The project was completed on the date that I had projected, and we all went on to complete several more important projects after that with very little altercation ever again.*

By now you are getting the idea. If, however, you are able to recall only a situation in which your work was criticized, begin with a caveat that it was never a major matter (unless it really was and even then don't emphasize it). Then, when you provide a brief scenario, it is not one in which you really made a major error of poor judgment. Also try to select a situation in which, even though initially you were overruled, sooner or later good judgment and your insight prevailed. The only thing left is not to hammer the point home at the expense of your adversaries. Try to show win-win. If you didn't win, it was no big deal for you and it is best to convey the impression that you did not take it personally.

☆ 3.14 There appears to be a gap of x months/years on your resume? What were you doing during this time?

You will be prepared to respond to this question if you take the time before the meeting to consider your activities both on and off the job. **Make your answer crisp, brief, focused on the point, and not defensive.** That kind of answer portrays you as a person who does what you have to do.

> *Constant care of a family member required someone's attention and the choice was between my spouse and myself. Because she had just started a new career, I decided to volunteer for the assignment.*

☆ 3.15 Do you have any objections to psychological testing? Testing for honesty? Drugs? Others?

If you have none, say so directly. The employer is asking probably because one or more tests are part of their selection process. In a few instances an employer may ask the question not because they have any of those tests, but because they feel that, by asking the question, applicants may screen themselves out. If you have objections to any or all of them—and you want to say so—be ready to describe your reason for the objection.

> *I object to psychological testing because I have learned that more often than not the results are either unreliable or invalid and sometimes they are both.*
>
> *I object to honesty tests because they are frequently personally intrusive. Is that true of the test you give here?*
>
> *I do not object to drug testing but I need to be sure you are aware that I am taking medication that may affect the results.*

☆ 3.16 What is the worst thing you ever heard about our organization/about working here?

Depending on the organization, this may be easy or difficult to answer. First of all, the principle of disclosure makes you shine or falter. Let's assume that the organization is in the news with bad press. Your not being aware of the news leads the interviewer to believe either that you are not knowledgeable about current events or (and it is hard to tell which is worse) that you do not wish to admit your knowledge. If the law has been broken, the organization has been found guilty and subject to fines and other penalties, and all this is public knowledge, state what you know. Then listen carefully to the comments the interviewer makes. By doing so, you show empathy and that is appreciated.

If the matter has not been resolved or is a matter of hearsay, be careful and practice answering this question before the interview in the presence of a trusted colleague or two to determine how much to share and withhold. If you have heard gossip and innuendo, repeat not one word. If the worst you have heard is that the competition for jobs at the organization is fierce because it is a terrific company—and you can say it with a straight face—that could be a sharp response.

3.17 *Have you ever been accused of sexual harassment?*

At first glance you may say that the question is not fair because the question says "accused" and not "found guilty of." (When we discuss illegal questions in Chap. 12, you will see that there are more legal protections for felonies than there are for sexual harassment. When pursuing an applicant's conviction record, interviewers are not allowed to ask, *"Have you ever been arrested?"*) Mary Gambardella, a labor attorney and partner with the law firm Epstein Becker and Green, states that the *interviewer not only has the right to ask but in fact should raise the question of sexual harassment if "... there is reason to believe there may have been a problem with the person being interviewed."* However, she also cautions that once the question is asked, if the answer is "that the person being considered has been found to have engaged in sexual harassment with past employers, there is an obligation not to hire that candidate." So if you happen to be interviewed by an organization that has received this kind of advice, chances are that the question will be raised. (See also page 167.) Even though the organization may ask this question and extend it to accusations, you need and have a right to protect yourself. If you have been accused of sexual harassment but ultimately exonerated, it is wiser to provide only a no answer because to provide any additional details will only put you at the mercy of the interviewer. Remember, to be accused of a crime does not indicate guilt in our society; so the same should be true for sexual harassment.

⭐ 3.18 *How does this position compare with others you are considering?*

If you mention others, then you have disclosed, perhaps without realizing it, that you may not have been as interested in this position as you led the interviewer to believe. On the other hand, if you answer that you are considering only this position, then the interviewer realizes that you have little or no choice. The unasked question is why not?

You may start by hedging, *"This is a unique position because it...."* Continue by describing the position in its own terms and in the organizational context. By keeping your answer to the position being discussed, you are neither admitting nor denying the existence of other opportunities under consideration.

3.19   Do you prefer staff or line work?

These terms date back to the military with *line* relating to an organization's essential functions while *staff* are support functions.

With the rise of the knowledge-based organization, line and staff distinctions blur. Organizations are recognizing the essential contribution of each participant; the thinking is that each must do its part on an equal basis for the organization to succeed. No function is greater or lesser than any other. The best answer, especially if you do not know the specifics of the available position is that you are able to perform effectively in either role, citing examples from your work history. If, of course, you know about the position, you might show that you are able to perform in either function but that you are particularly adept in specified functions.

3.20   What is your overall impression of your current/last job [... of your current/last organization]?

These are easy questions to deal with. Be upbeat and professional but do not sugar coat anything.

> *It was a great opportunity for personal growth. After three years of doing the same thing and a downturn in the industry, I saw the handwriting on the wall and that is why I am looking now.*

> *I was fortunate to have the opportunity to work with such a great group of dedicated professionals. Unfortunately, technology passed them by and the management of the organization has yet to respond to the challenge of a changed market.*

☆ 3.21   Can we contact your references, present/former employers?

If you are presently employed, you certainly do not want your employers knowing about your job search until you have given notice. State, *"I will be very pleased to provide excellent references from my current employer if a position is offered. If you wish to contact any of my former employers please let me know before you do so."* It is a mark of professional courtesy for you to notify any of the references that you have provided of the names and organizations that will be contacting them.

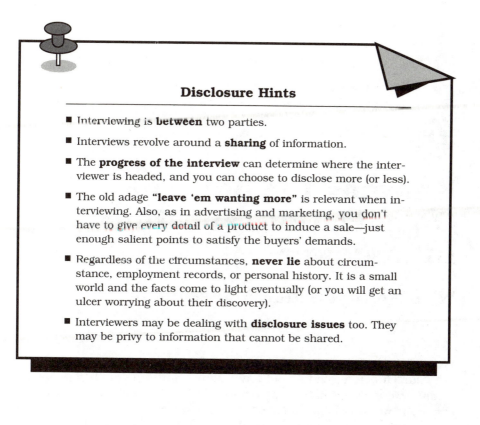

Disclosure Hints

- Interviewing is **between** two parties.

- Interviews revolve around a **sharing** of information.

- The **progress of the interview** can determine where the interviewer is headed, and you can choose to disclose more (or less).

- The old adage **"leave 'em wanting more"** is relevant when interviewing. Also, as in advertising and marketing, you don't have to give every detail of a product to induce a sale—just enough salient points to satisfy the buyers' demands.

- Regardless of the circumstances, **never lie** about circumstance, employment records, or personal history. It is a small world and the facts come to light eventually (or you will get an ulcer worrying about their discovery).

- Interviewers may be dealing with **disclosure issues** too. They may be privy to information that cannot be shared.

4

Knowing the Job, the Organization, and Your Interviewer

What Are You Getting Yourself into?

What job are *you* looking for? This is one of the first questions you should ask yourself before sending out any resumes and certainly before going on any interviews. What exactly do you want from a job? What are your employment-related "must haves," "be nice to haves," and "definitely do not wants"? If those who do not study history are condemned to repeat it, then a wise move is to analyze your work history. Much of the time preparing for interviews and undergoing interviews revolves around self-analysis. So let's get started.

Looking at your current resume, what did you like about your past jobs? Using the Job History Worksheet, list your current and past jobs and what you liked and did not like about each job. Some of the likes and dislikes may be inherent in the job itself and are probably found in any organization, but others may change with the territory.

What did you learn from the list? Keep those likes and dislikes in mind as we turn from the past into the future.

What kind of an organization do you want to work for? Of the 11 million businesses out there, many will suit your individual needs. The trick is to recognize what you want in your next job. Do you like working for a big company or small? Do you prefer structured or free flowing reporting? The questionnaire, My Ideal Job (page 38), helps you focus on your preferred choices.

Job History Worksheet		
Job: **Organization and** **description**	**Likes:** **The best parts** **of the job**	**Dislikes:** **The worst parts** **of the job**

My Ideal Job

Circle your preferences.

The organization will be	small/large.
It will be in	a large city/a small town/the suburbs.
It should be within	50/100+ miles of my home.
It will be in the business of	service/products.
The business will be	a start-up/well established.
The business will be	publicly owned/private/government/not-for-profit.
The organization will be	conservative/avant garde.
My position will require supervising others	a lot/somewhat/not at all.
I would like to work	on a team all the time/ with others sometimes/ alone most of the time.
I want to be supervised	closely/intermittently/from a distance.
I want to work with the public	all the time/from time to time/seldom.
My job should be	high tech/low tech/no tech.
I prefer to work with	people/things/data.
I prefer to work	on the phone/face-to-face/both.
I prefer to	delegate/do it myself.
My new job should be	same as old/different.
My work pace should be	slow/steady/busy or fast.
I want to be paid	a salary/commissions.
I want to travel	a lot/sometimes/never.
I want to work	in a big office/in a small office/ in my own office/at home.
My weekly schedule should be	40 hours+/20–30 hours/ part time/flexible.
I am available	for overtime/weekends.

Additionally, although salary is extremely important, often all those additional benefits can make or break a job offer. What are your basic requirements? Is on-site child care or flextime a necessity? Which is more important to you, retirement benefits or a dental plan? How important is a liberal tuition refund policy? What other benefits would you add to a wish list? Use the form, My New Job Must Have (page 40), to list your requirements.

Complete the Personal Worksheet (pages 41–42) next to look at all the things that make you unique. The last sections of the form ask you to look at what you really like to do and why. If you really like to program computers but are looking for a position as a supervisor, this is time for a reality check. Perhaps supervisor positions pay more, or maybe there is a glut of programmers in the area. But if you love programming because of the detailed hands-on work and creativity, will you also love supervising programmers? Can you "sell" yourself as a supervisor? Compensation and financial needs are legitimate reasons for taking "less than perfect" jobs as long as you are honest with yourself about your motivations.

Now, using the information from all four worksheets, write a description of your targeted job and ideal organization on an index card, as shown in the following sample. This is your "wish list" to refer to throughout your job search. Notice that it is written on paper, not in stone. Make adjustments as needed. You should also determine what level of compensation is needed. You may have additional travel expenses if your job search extends outside your immediate area, or you may no longer be able to car pool to the office. How much money do you need? Then, as you review various job offers and benefit packages, you must evaluate how much each position should pay.

<u>Ideal job</u> will be in a large, international corporation headquartered in city within 90-minute commute from my home. I like high tech., innovative, private company. I can work weekends and travel as needed; great working with others in person and on phone. Love to have own office but not needed; hate big offices with cubbies.

Must have good medical/dental plan; profit sharing a plus. Not interested in retirement benefits now.

<u>Position:</u> supervise 10–15 programmers, make own dept. hiring decisions & budget; love to design new programs

Sal. $85–95,000

My New Job Must Have ...

Deal makers: *List those perks/benefits that you must have in any new job offers.*

_____

_____

_____

_____

_____

_____

_____

_____

_____

_____

Deal sweeteners: *List any perks/benefits that it would be nice to have.*

_____

_____

_____

_____

_____

_____

_____

_____

_____

Personal Worksheet

What I am like: *List all the adjectives that can be used to describe you. Some examples are given but add your own.*

Aggressive	Calm	Cheerful	Cooperative
Creative	Dependable	Efficient	Flexible
Generous	Hardworking	Loyal	Methodical
Objective	Patient	Perceptive	Punctual
Sensitive	Terse	Uninhibited	Vibrant

What I can do: *List all the things you can accomplish. Examples are given but add your own.*

Administer	Advise	Assign	Check
Compute	Coordinate	Delegate	Design
Evaluate	File	Identify	Initiate
Lead	Negotiate	Plan	Problem solve
Reason	Summarize	Test	Update

Personal Worksheet (continued)

What I know: *List everything that you know about, either through work or school or outside interests. Some examples are given but add your own.*

Accounting	Art	Bookkeeping	Benefits
Computers	Economics	Electronics	Editing
Finance	Geography	Graphics	Health care
History	Language	Literature	Music
Programming	Repair	Selling	Writing

What I really like to do: *Of all the things that you know and that you can do, list, in order of preference, the top ten things you would like to do in your new job.*

1.
2.
3.
4.
5.
6.
7.
8.
9.
10.

Why? *List the reasons why you picked the top five preferences.*

1.
2.
3.
4.
5.

Reality Check

As stated elsewhere, it is not necessarily the best candidate who gets the job, but usually the best interviewee. Make that the best *informed* interviewee. Go to the library and look up any information available about your target organization. Reference books and directories, such as those published by Standard & Poor's, Dun and Bradstreet, Dow Jones (with an on-line directory), Moody's Investors' Service, and Polk's, as well as periodicals and industry publications, can prove to be of great assistance.

❑ At what types of organizations are you interviewing?

❑ Are they private or publicly traded?

❑ Are they international or local?

❑ How long have they been in business?

❑ What exactly is their business?

❑ How many employees are on-site?

❑ Who are their competitors?

❑ How big are they?

❑ How has business been lately?

❑ How do they conduct their business?

❑ What major trends or problems might affect them?

If appropriate, call up the organization and request a recent annual report or any other publications. Use the Organization Fact Sheet (page 44) to gather facts about the organization. You can create a "file" by attaching any articles or additional information regarding the organization or the industry. Other questions are:

❑ How did you learn of this job opening?

❑ How long has the job been open?

❑ What is the job description?

❑ What about salary and benefits?

Now, look at your "ideal" organization on your index card. How close are you? Do you have enough information? What additional information do you need? On another Need to Know index card (page 45) list information to be gathered prior to your interview or questions to ask at the interview itself. As you get additional information, add it to your file or Organization Fact Sheet. By the time you go to the interview, you should have gone through several versions of the index card with only a few points left to be covered.

Organization Fact Sheet

Name:

Address: _____

Telephone: _____

Directions: _____

Contact person: _____

   Title: _____   Telephone number: _____

   Office location: _____

   Referred by: _____

   How contacted: _____

Business: _____

_____

Started in: _____

Number of employees: _____

Number of locations/sites: _____

Ownership: _____

Senior management: _____

_____

Recent sales/earnings: _____

What has been trend past 5 years? _____

_____

Markets: _____

Market share: _____

Leading competitors: _____

Trends/recent developments: _____

Other information: _____

_____

Position: Job title: _____

   Description: _____

   Major responsibilities: _____

   Size of unit: _____

   Location of unit: _____

   Salary range: _____

   Reports to/supervisor: _____

   Other information: _____

```
Need to know:
How long position open? (lots of turnover?)
Does marketing report directly to President? If not, who to?
Physical offices: rumor that it's cramped for space?? Visit??
Finances? Privately held!! How are they doing?
Size of department's annual budget/staffing requirements? When
is budget done (will I get to do it??)
Organization chart: others on "my" level?
How is department viewed by senior management? Do they
like current ad campaigns or are they planning to outsource
in future? What % spent annually in various media? Looking
to keep same or diversify?
```

Experience vs. Potential: Which One Matters?

Which is more important, experience or potential? A recruiter for a major New York City global money center remarked that one of the frustrating aspects of the job search process is that, depending on the background and role of the interviewer, either one might matter more than the other. The issue is of such importance because, depending on the interviewer and his or her organizational position, one is so much more important over the other that in every situation, experience or potential will be considered exclusively over the other. Frequently, personnel/human resource professionals assume a "holier than the pope" role and insist on screening for only those candidates that meet the line manager's job requirements to a "t." Line managers are, on the other hand, usually more liberal in considering candidates. Fit and attractiveness (i.e., total presentation) may be weighed more heavily than skill level and actual experience. The comparison on the following page gives you some insight into which matters more, depending on who is interviewing you.

Kinds of Interviews

Screening Interviews

Whether you are presenting yourself to an agency, a recruiter, or an HR department, you will be subject to a certain number of screening interviews. The "gatekeepers" doing the interview have basic information regarding

Which Matters More?	
Experience	**Potential**
Interviewed by HR	Interviewed by line personnel
Looking to match criteria, screening candidates	Assumes criteria match, looks to "fit" the position
Concerned about internal credibility	Concerned with solving problem.

the job opening and the requirements for the position. Their function is to pass on only those candidates who appear to fit the position. They ask direct questions about your experience, education, expectations. They go over your resume with you. Depending on the experience level of the interviewer, you may be interviewed in depth. But it is of no matter that this is a low-level interview: if you do not pass the gatekeepers, then you are out. Their job is to weed out those who are inappropriate for the position. Those who "pass" proceed to another level at the organization or, if the gatekeeper was an agency or recruiter, to the hiring organization.

Courtesy Interviews

You know when you have one of these. You've gotten a lead, called in your markers, and gotten into the organization to see if they have anything for you. You may be referred by a present employee, a client, a relative, or a neighbor—anyone who has a tie-in to the company and who could get your foot in the door. Be thankful that you are there because organizations realize that their best employees are referred to them. Supposedly your lead knows you and the organization, and thinks it may be a good match. Pursue this line in your interview. This interview may be similar in tone to a screening interview (they may not know what to do with you), but it can be extremely important in getting a line on a job that may be opening up soon or on a referral to another interview.

Stress Interviews

They exist. Unless you are looking to be head of a major urban transit system, school chancellor, or any position so inundated with stress that mere mortals need not apply, stress interviews are not common. There are ways to deal with them, as covered in detail in Chap. 10.

Situational Interviews

Can you think on your feet? These interviews involve behavioral questions, such as *"Let's pretend ..."* and *"What if ..."* scenarios. The interviewer may be either trying out real-life problems on you to see what you would do or just may be in a creative mood. The interviewer is looking for empathy: Can you put yourself into another's place? How would you act? If you have the knowledge and experience on paper, the interviewer can take you on a miniroad test to see how you run with these types of questions. After you are done you might want to comment, *"Those were really intriguing questions. Do they relate to real-life situations here at _____?"*

Team Interviews

You may be faced with several interviewers at the same time, with either one taking the lead and the others interjecting from time to time, or you may face a battery of questions from all directions. This could border on a stress interview if the interview goes out of control. Treat each question one at a time and listen carefully.

An organization that has this type of interview approach may be signaling its priorities loud and clear. Before you leave, you might inquire as to their reasons for this approach (*"Was it you or do they do this all the time?"*). It is okay to be inquisitive; just do not ask in a judgmental tone.

Kinds of Interviewers

Terrific, Prepared Professionals

This is the interviewer for whom you have prepared and with whom you hope to meet. However, as with any group of people that lends itself to statistical analysis, the truly great interviewers are the exception rather than the rule. It is a really memorable experience to meet one of these individuals, regardless of the outcome. You will find that the interview is a challenging but really probing conversation. You depart feeling that you had an opportunity to provide a complete picture to the interviewer of who you are (as it relates to the position for which you are under consideration). You take away information about yourself that you had either forgotten or were never aware of. When you prepare for any meeting, prepare, be ready, and set your sights to meet with this individual. Prepared, well trained, and experienced interviewers are also the most challenging. If they are prepared, they expect you to be as well. If you are not, it is not a very rewarding or pleasant experience for you.

Well-Trained But Negative and Burned out

This interviewer is well trained and highly experienced, but has seen better days. You can identify these individuals because they share inappropriate information with the candidate (*"I don't know why you or anyone else would want to work here."*). They may give a stress interview because they happen to feel this is what gets them through the day, or they may show disinterest in the applicant's answers. Do not write this interview off. Take advantage of this willingness to share negative information, and consider whether the interviewer is sharing with you reasons for personal dissatisfaction.

Well Trained But Inexperienced

This interviewer may be new to the field and may have just completed very good training. This arrangement works if the applicant is not complicated and does not have a variety of information that the interviewer does not know how to process. The applicant should be extra careful to stay within the parameters established by the questions and provide simple, direct answers. A very experienced job applicant must be careful to avoid patronizing this type of interviewer or demonstrating frustration for any reason. Anticipated perceptions of the interviewer might turn out to be at variance with the reality of the situation. If you demonstrate any of these feelings, the interviewer will see it, and you will have diminished the possibility for success.

Well Trained But Incompetent

This is a terrible situation. This interviewer controls access to the organization, and the applicant is dependent on the person to set up the meetings. The problem is like an "Alice in Wonderland" interview: You don't know what will happen or where it is going. The applicant may detect the level of training of the interviewer from the questions asked and their sequence. Yet any analysis of the dynamics of the situation indicates that the interviewer is either a poor listener or going through the motions without really understanding the process (asking redundant questions, or giving strange verbal cues such as smiling during a discussion about a termination story or a personal tragedy). In this situation, listen carefully to identify any positive signals from the interviewer. Then stay focused on that area of inquiry or interest with simple direct answers, watching to ensure a high level of support from the interviewer.

Well Trained But Unprepared

In this situation the interviewer may very well start with your favorite *"Tell me a little about yourself"* or *"Give me a moment to review your resume. I haven't had a chance to review it before now and I didn't want to delay the process."* These interviewers become focused and evaluate candidates using all their listening skills. Do not write off this interviewer, but be patient and try to recognize opportunities to "ring the bell" with your responses. Mention something that strikes a responsive chord with these interviewers, and in all likelihood they will suddenly become very focused and attentive. If the situation really feels out of hand, you may ask, *"Is this still a good time for you?"* or *"Would it be more convenient to reschedule?"* Avoid making a big deal of the interviewer's lack of preparation.

Well Trained But Distracted

This person seems like a good interviewer, but for some reason your comments are not having any impact. You need to determine the reason for the distraction. In this situation persistence eventually pays off … or not. Whatever you do, do not take the distractedness personally. Something outside the interview process may have just had an impact on the interviewer, something you are powerless to do anything about. You may seriously consider asking something like, *"Are you okay?"* or *"Shall I continue?"* You may also consider adding the comment, *"You seem preoccupied. Perhaps we should continue this meeting at a time more convenient for you."* And wait for the response. The responses range from total denial to total agreement. Regardless of the response, a reasonable person appreciates your attention and concern. The outcome is recognition for your sensitivity to another and that is not taken in a negative way. You can also provide cues to move the interview along the right track by rephrasing questions to call attention to your answer, *"Since you asked about my management experience, I would like to point out that, in addition to being in charge of my unit for the past three years, I have also taught classes in management at _____ University."*

Poorly Trained

This is a tough situation because everyone loses. The organization does not bring back the best candidates for a second meeting, and the candidate is dropped because an interviewer feels it is easier to say no than to look diligently for reasons to say yes to your candidacy.

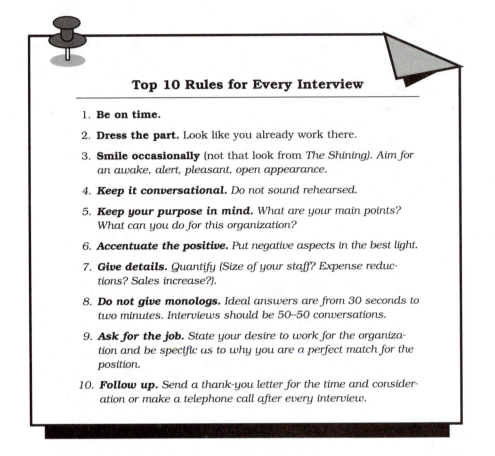

Top 10 Rules for Every Interview

1. **Be on time.**

2. **Dress the part.** Look like you already work there.

3. **Smile occasionally** (not that look from *The Shining*). Aim for an awake, alert, pleasant, open appearance.

4. *Keep it conversational.* Do not sound rehearsed.

5. *Keep your purpose in mind.* What are your main points? What can you do for this organization?

6. *Accentuate the positive.* Put negative aspects in the best light.

7. *Give details.* Quantify (Size of your staff? Expense reductions? Sales increase?).

8. *Do not give monologs.* Ideal answers are from 30 seconds to two minutes. Interviews should be 50–50 conversations.

9. *Ask for the job.* State your desire to work for the organization and be specific as to why you are a perfect match for the position.

10. *Follow up.* Send a thank-you letter for the time and consideration or make a telephone call after every interview.

5

Small Talk Questions

Breaking the Ice

Small talk is the lubricant of social interaction. It is something that can be used (and perfected) in a variety of situations—personal and professional. People who demonstrate a facility for small talk inevitably impress everyone they meet. Even the few who detest small talk may begrudge the small talk experts their facility with words.

Face-to-face conversation is something that has been reduced in importance with the inventions of the TV, telephone, and computer. Before the arrival of TV, people had to be active participants in the listening process because face-to-face conversation (and even radio) demanded that the listener participate in the process. The listener was required to actively participate in the message being sent. Concentration on what was being heard was essential because that was the only way to receive the message.

With the arrival of TV, receivers of the message could be much more laid back because the visual image gives viewers two opportunities now to "hear" what was said. First, they can take in the aural message. Second, they can absorb the visual images on the screen. Additionally, recent television programming has been a major factor in changes in the way people communicate because of the importance television places on its need to entertain while it is sending messages. Even with the inundation of "talk" shows, there is very little "small talk." The host dives into the hot topic of the day! Communication and interaction have been reduced in many ways to "sound bites."

The Problem with Most Small Talk—You Need an Agenda

The problem with most small talk is that the persons involved are not aware of a basic but essential element of small talk: It must proceed with a clearly defined agenda if it is to be effective.

The most natural "agendas" for small talk in a supermarket line are those that you feel common to others around you: long wait, sale items, high prices, favorite cashier. We have all found ourselves in similar circumstances—stuck on long airplane flights, delayed trains, doctor or dentist offices—when chatting with others (or being chatted to) is one way to pass the time. We have all met people for the first time and sought for ways to make them feel welcome and comfortable. In the interview process, **small talk is one way to break the ice and establish some rapport. The interviewer hopes to unlock your deepest secrets in the search for the "perfect" hire.**

Another problem with small talk is that we are our own worst critics. It is easy to say, "I just can't chat about nothing." That may be tantamount to saying that you just do not want to make the effort or risk doing it less than adequately. You may be one of many people who hates small talk for a variety of reasons, but the most common, according to experts on the topic, is that we feel we are terrible at it. Small talk is an art form that is fun to use and should be a skill practiced whenever possible throughout our lives. The more you do it, the better you get at it.

Effective small talk in the interview process, while triggering your active listening mode, achieves two important objectives:

1. Allows the organization to appear to be **"people-oriented"** through personal attention to the candidate.

2. Sets a **tone of goodwill and positive feelings** that enhances the interview and encourages the applicant to relax and be more open.

Interviewers have a responsibility to the organization to screen in all the candidates that they feel are serious candidates who meet the qualifications for the position—possessing the knowledge, skills, abilities to do the job, along with the motivation—and who are interpersonal "fits." If the tone is set properly, the organization and its representatives are accomplishing their objective: **to learn as much as they can about the person without being exceedingly intrusive.**

You Arrive for the Interview

Look for small talk opportunities. You may be the initiator or you may not. Once physically in the organization, you are more likely to come in contact with people assigned to the department you are meeting with. Use the opportunity to "warm up" by getting a feeling for the temperament of those working for the organization.

These oral exchanges also warm up your listening skills. "Ice-breakers" should trigger your listening skills and get you set for the real business of the interview. This is particularly important early in the day because you may have spent all your time and effort since rising virtually "talking to yourself" and getting ready for this meeting. The more you make conscientious attempts to hear and listen to what is going on around you, the more prepared you are when the interview commences to listen to what is being said.

You can initiate small talk too. You are not confined to responding to questions. This may be an opportunity to comment on an article in a periodical read in the waiting area—whether the subject was organization-related or not. If the person you are meeting with (or the department) is mentioned, certainly give it a try without being obsequious. *"Your department played a major role in the organization's annual blood drive. I can appreciate what it took to take responsibility for that project because when I was at XYZ Enterprises I participated in our blood drive for five years in a row."* This is then the opportunity for the interviewer to ask a follow-up question (such as *"Oh, did you have to arrange the kick-off dinner as well?"*) and to search for similarities in approach and challenges.

Avoid Controversial Topics at All Costs

If the article that caught your eye addresses a strike (settled or not) at the organization, wait until later to raise the matter (if it needs to be addressed at all). Also watch out for hot topics unrelated to the organization.

5.1 *What a beautiful/miserable/cold/hot/rainy/windy day, isn't it?*

This is a giveaway. Don't get into a dialog worthy only of the weather channel. Even in these controversial times, people can still agree that there is nothing to do about the weather.

5.2 *Did you have a hard time finding the building/our office? Did your plane come in on time? How is your hotel?*

Consider very carefully your responses to any questions about your arrival if they included travel arrangements that the organization provided. You want to avoid commenting negatively on anyone's weak performance and shedding unfavorable light on your own situation. In the worst situation of totally boggled flights and reservations, you are not seen in an unfavorable light if you comment that *"The arrangements were just perfect and I got here without a hitch."* With that comment you accomplish two things: You pretty much close the discussion on the topic extremely quickly since you are hoping to move on to more important issues (namely yourself and their job opening) and the tone you set is totally positive. It is a small issue, and you pay a compliment to those responsible. You cannot lose with that response. If the interviewer has had totally terrible experiences with the same group, the worst he or she can do is indicate that and perhaps add surprise at the results you obtained. But you are not faulted regardless. If you had problems and if you feel they need to be brought up at all, try to minimize them. You need to put this question behind you in a positive way so that you can get to the real questions that need time to be given to your important answers.

However, *if you were late for the interview* (due to their misdirections or your own errors), keep the problems to yourself. Apologize quickly (this may have been their agenda in raising the question) and accept the responsibility for the lateness yourself. *"I know I am late. I am terribly sorry. I should have anticipated more of a delay during rush hour. If I have inconvenienced you, let me suggest a new date and I promise you I will be on time."*

These type of questions may be inserted at the beginning, and you may lead off by disclosing an item that begs for a response. For example, in response to, **"Did you have trouble finding us?"** your response may be *"No, because my chess club frequently meets in the building across the street."* The interviewer then has an opportunity to ask a follow-up question such as, **"Oh, are you a serious chess player?"** Inserting this kind of data personally, instead of on your resume, allows you to be spontaneous and take advantage of any "clues" in the office of the interviewer (a chess set in the far corner of the bookshelf or photo of him or her at a chess tournament).

5.3 What about those Rangers/the City Council election/the paving of the Interstate?

Presumably your job search has not precluded your reading newspapers or watching news programs. If you are traveling to another city, try to read a local paper in advance to determine what is in the news. Besides being up on local issues, a local newspaper provides insight into the area both as a possible place for you to move to and as the arena where the organization itself plays. **The more you know about how and where the organization operates, the better prepared you are.**

5.4 I saw on your resume that you enjoy _____. How did you get interested in this?

This question demonstrates two things:

1. **You control the data** that you wish to share.

2. Once you provide the data on the resume, it is **fair game** for a line of inquiry.

Give a brief reason that answers the question. Consider it in advance so that it shows that you just don't haphazardly jump into things. At the same time phrase the answer to imply that you are always open to the new and different but that golf or coin collecting never gets into the way of job performance.

Including this type of information may be more trouble than it's worth. Why take the risk of exposing yourself as a charlatan on a job-irrelevant issue like hobbies or special interests when there is no reason to if you run into an argumentative "expert." Second, why lift your apprehension for the meeting because you have to worry whether the person you are dealing with is an expert on the subject or hates your hobby or you are perceived as too caught up in your outside activities to concentrate on the job at hand!

5.5 I see that you also went to _____ (school). How is Professor _____ these days? I see you went to _____. I went there myself. Do they still _____?

Share the answer if you know it. If you do not, admit it without apology but with a brief explanation of why you do not know. The interviewer should understand that, even though you and a favorite instructor were at XYZ University at the same time, you may never have taken the course or even recognize the name. Do not go on the defensive, pretend you know when you don't, and have to worry about the next question. If you keep up with the alumni or have a family member attending the school, briefly share this with the interviewer. Again, you have no idea as to whether the interviewer had a good time at the school or not. So do not enthuse or complain about your alma mater; you may risk landing on the wrong side of the issue.

5.6 How do you like living in _____?

Be positive. Even if it is the worst place in the world, try in advance to identify something about it that can be mentioned in an attractive light. If the place is controversial (for example, New York City or Detroit) and you wish to hedge your answer, give a balanced opinion such as, *"It's a* *terrific place because you don't need a car but it has more than its share of hassles from a business perspective."* By making the statement and being brief, you are showing your interest in addressing the question directly and giving it importance because the interviewer has determined it is important enough to ask. While answering, watch interviewers for non-verbal clues to determine whether they agree or disagree. If they have heard enough, the line of questioning ends there. If they want to know more and your reply has stirred more interest, they will continue with a follow-up question.

Watch, too, for a sneaky hint of the originator's bias in the communication of the question. This question may be loaded with prejudice. If the location has a reputation for high crime or high incidences of a social problem (e.g., drugs) or disease (e.g., there is a community on Long Island with a higher than normal rate of cancer among its residents), there could be a hidden agenda.

5.7 I see that you are reading _____ (book/magazine/paper). Do you get to read often?

Just as we mentioned when discussing the inclusion of interests and hobbies on the resume, you control what you do share with the interviewer through oral and written communication. Don't forget disclosure goes beyond that. Your whole appearance sends a message. That includes anything that you carry with you (bag, briefcase, and anything in them that you take out and show to anyone during the process).

If you want to show you read *The Economist* (and/or *The Wall Street Journal*), bring a copy and read it while waiting. The same is true for any other publication or book. Once you choose to use it, you are fair game to be tested on your knowledge of it. Be wary of publications when interviewing in the publishing field; you do not want to advertise the competition's attraction. The same could be true of fashions, fragrance, and jewelry.

5.8 I see that you drive a _____. How is it?

This question indicates two things about interviewers. First, they want to show that they noticed the vehicle you are driving.

Second, they want you to know that they recognized it and thought it important enough to ask you a question about it. Whether or not the only purpose for the question is to take it as an opportunity to ask a small talk question to set you at ease, treat it as such and be brief and to the point. If it is the worst car you have ever owned, do not let on. Be positive. If the car has a terrible reputation (deserved or not), consider borrowing someone else's vehicle for the meeting. Some people measure others by the vehicle they drive (or the place they live); the vehicle chosen becomes one more opportunity to judge the choice made by the applicant. If you are applying for a job with an organization in the automobile industry, consider whether your vehicle is regarded as belonging to the competition.

5.9   Our team has won the industry cup for three years in a row. Do you play _____?

If your resume says you do, the question should be a "no-brainer." On the other hand, you may take this as an opportunity to qualify your level of performance. Be realistic and do not apologize. If you are aware of the quality and or level of play at this organization and you feel you are able to join the team, say so. Organizations that take their sports seriously may choose between you and another candidate who does not play based on that. If you do not play, express an interest in watching a game, if appropriate. Inquire as to where and when they play. Does the interviewer play? If you are sincere, ask if you can attend a game.

5.10   What do you prefer to be called?

This is a considerate question that indicates the interviewer wishes to make you comfortable by calling you the way you wished to be called. With today's diversity, even a common name like Matthew is a name that has three alternatives: Matthew, Matt, and Mattie. Interviewers show their concern by acknowledging that something as direct as a name is not to be taken for granted. If you really prefer one version over others and it is important to you, even if the question is not asked, mention it. **Your name is important to you and you get to determine the impact it has on the interviewer.** Interviewers who cannot say your name as requested, even after you mention it, may be poor listeners, and your meeting therefore is unfortunately highly suspect. Why not find that out sooner rather than later and adjust your sights accordingly.

One more comment: If your name is so important to you, don't forget to share that information as soon as you can, including taking the opportunity before the meeting. Your correspondence and even your resume could easily contain the derivative or nickname that you very strongly prefer. If your nickname is a little on the cutesy side (Bucky, Dee-Dee), consider strongly the image you are projecting and the tone of the organization you are presenting yourself to (shirtsleeves or three-piece suits, "Chanel" or "Betsey Johnson") before sharing this. If hired, you can always reveal your alter identity to those you choose.

5.11   What do you think about (any controversial "in the news" topic)?

This is a question that may crop up during the small talk portion of the interview. It is a chance for the interviewer to see if you are keeping up with current events, or it may just be friendly banter on a topic that you would have to be dead to have no knowledge about. *The commencement of this seemingly innocuous line of inquiry may provide an opportunity for interviewers to probe into your beliefs and political opinions to determine if those views are acceptable.* Show that you are informed but try to avoid taking sides, before and after interviewers reveal their views of the issue—if they choose to do so. By staying above giving an opinion, you are sustaining a "mystique" and you make interviewers keep trying to determine who you are. If the mystery of who you are is gone, interviewers may go through the motions but they have heard enough and already formed an opinion. If you make them work to get insight into who you are, you sustain interest and grow positively in their opinion because they are required to make judgments regarding who you are. The more they have to work to make those determinations, the more they develop a positive impression.

5.12   Would you like something to drink? A cigarette?

Some cultures use an offer of a drink as an opportunity to demonstrate hospitality. Others use it to determine the astuteness of the candidate (the acceptance of the drink may be a test to determine the applicant's professional sophistication because in some cultures a drink is accepted only after a relationship is established). **Do not become hung up on the more weighty aspects and hidden meanings of the issue.** Even if you want a cup of coffee (in fact, you are dying for one), pass on it politely. This is not a social call.

Some applicants, however, use the offer as one more indicator and opportunity to evaluate the organization. Whether they use porcelain cups or Styrofoam, real milk or chemical substitute, remember you are not there to evaluate the quality of the beverage but to get a job.

The issue of smoking in the office may be decided ahead of time by local statues and clean air laws. If you are traveling to another geographical area and may be unaware of local statutes, observe the presence or lack of ashtrays and signage. One tobacco manufacturer has a "Thank You for Smoking" sign in the lobby! If you are a nonsmoker and the air is blue with smoke, you may have gotten your first indication of whether you wish to work in that environment.

The same goes for other inquiries such as, *"Where did you get that suit?" "Wow—what a great tan. Where did you go?" "I am so backed up [looking at a desk full of printouts]—don't you just hate computers?"* Small talk can be a great assist to your job search and can be helpful regardless of the setting. Whether you are in the beginning of an interview or en route to an appointment, you never know where the opportunity may arise to uncover a job prospect that may develop from casual conversation started with a person that just happens to be standing next to you. One comment may lead to another, and, before you realize it (sly fox that you are), you have disclosed that you are looking for a job. The stranger, with whom you have just started the most casual of conversations, is aware of an open position. Not only might you pursue it, but you should use his or her name.

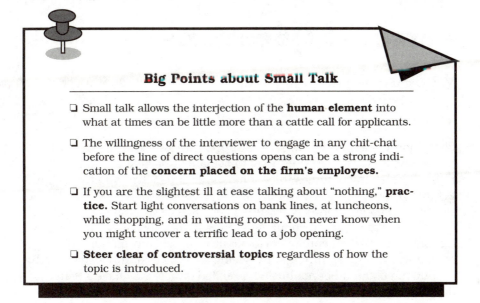

Big Points about Small Talk

❏ Small talk allows the interjection of the **human element** into what at times can be little more than a cattle call for applicants.

❏ The willingness of the interviewer to engage in any chit-chat before the line of direct questions opens can be a strong indication of the **concern placed on the firm's employees.**

❏ If you are the slightest ill at ease talking about "nothing," **practice.** Start light conversations on bank lines, at luncheons, while shopping, and in waiting rooms. You never know when you might uncover a terrific lead to a job opening.

❏ **Steer clear of controversial topics** regardless of how the topic is introduced.

6
Personal Questions

Who Are You?

For a long while interviewers were supposed to stick to the straight and narrow when it came to questions to ask a prospective candidate. (Civil rights legislation continues to be a harsh reminder that employers could get into trouble when straying from interview questions specifically and closely related to work.) Now, however, interviewers are interested in learning all that they can about every person they interview. They have a responsibility to their employers to obtain as much information about you as you are willing to provide. By seeing your likes and dislikes and by finding out about other nonbusiness-related issues, they have a better understanding of what you are about—on and off the job.

Personal questions are intended to allow the interviewer to get to understand another dimension of your make-up:

> *What has brought you into this particular interviewer's office?*
> *How has your job search been going?*
> *How had your career progressed up until this point?*
> *What are your feelings about this organization and this position?*

Measuring Your EQ

As highlighted recently in the media, an important ingredient for life success is emotional intelligence (EQ) [Daniel Coleman, *The New York Times* (September 10, 1995), Ideas and Trends, *The Decline of the Nice Guy Quotient*; Daniel Coleman, *Daily News,* USA Weekend (September 8–10, 1995), *The New Thinking on Smarts.* Both are excerpts from his book *Emotional In-*

telligence (Bantam)]. **Interpersonal skills are needed** to know and understand what you and others around you are feeling and to know how to handle those feelings skillfully:

> *How do you motivate others? Can you empathize with customers, clients, supervisors, fellow workers? Can you see another's point of view? When things get tough, boring, hectic, or chaotic at work, how do you react and how do you help others to manage their feelings? Can you defuse emotionally charged situations? Do you know what makes you happy?*

Employers, even before the term "emotional intelligence" was coined, knew that merely having the intelligence or the skill to perform a job was not sufficient. Some experts even go so far as to attach negative emotional attributes such as "cold," "calculating," "condescending," "inhibited," or "fastidious" to individuals with high IQs. On the other hand, individuals with high emotional abilities are seen as "cheerful," "sympathetic," "responsible," "ethical," or "committed" because they appear to be happy with themselves and the people they associate with.

This **emotional intelligence translates into better communication skills** on the job. Others want to work with and for people who understand them and who are able to support them. If fellow workers with high EQs have a problem, they are more likely to attract others to help solve the problem than someone with a low EQ. **One thing that you are selling is your ability to problem solve,** not just physical problems (coming up with a better mousetrap) but **interpersonal problems** as well (assembling the team that develops a better mousetrap).

Even if interviewers are not on the cutting edge of this latest philosophical theory, they know the organization needs individuals who work well together. The employment puzzle needs a good "fit" and personal questions are needed to find out what type of fit you would make.

To relate your EQ to the position and organization that you are interviewing for, refer to the Personal Worksheet (page 41) that you completed earlier. Looking at the first section (What I Am Like), list on the On-the-Job EQ Worksheet (page 62) the specific attributes that you feel the organization associates with the position. For example, a supervisor of programmers might need to be "objective," "adaptable," "efficient," "hardworking," and so forth for a position at a software developer whose business is just taking off (a baby Microsoft, perhaps). Give a specific example from your experience when you needed to be "objective":

> *When one of the designs I worked on was having problems, I had to refer it to another department to review the specs. The problem turned out not to be in the design but in a faulty component. Had I not referred it out but kept tinkering to fix it myself it would have taken longer to resolve the problem.*

On-the-Job EQ

Organization: _____

Position: _____

Personal attributes needed for this position:	Specific example of when/where you exhibited this attribute:

☆ 6.1　*Tell me about yourself.*

This is a terrible "question" whenever asked during an interview. The statement is usually made at the beginning of the formal part of the interview (and after the small talk/introductory phase, if it is going to be used at all). In some circumstances (not a job interview), it is a great opener (for counseling interviews in a highly nondirected setting), but this interviewing approach requires highly trained and seasoned interviewers to be utilized most effectively. It is very likely that interviewers using this approach are:

❏ Either **behind in the work that they had hoped to complete this day** and have just remembered a commitment to conduct this interview and/or have forgotten what they did with your resume and other paperwork.

❏ Or **have read somewhere** in a superficial periodical that this is a great way to start an interview and have decided to try the question.

Job seekers tell me that they are now interviewing for training programs that use a variation of this technique. *"Tell me, starting with school, and progressing through the jobs that you have held, about what you have been doing. Include any accomplishments, and bring me up to the present."* Even if this approach is used and the person you are facing has gone through extensive training, don't be lulled into thinking that he or she is any more prepared to turn your data into useful information than in the two other scenarios.

To know how to respond is important and to do so in two minutes or less is essential. Whether you put interviewers to sleep or not is not as important as being able to retain their attention. More than two minutes increases the possibility of either boring interviewers or losing their attention. In case this doesn't bother you, consider what you might have to do to awaken an interviewer who is fast asleep.

Take the time before the meeting to plan a script that you prepare precisely for such occasions. Some sample answers for different scenarios:

If you are reentering the job market after a time away:

I have experience in both the not-for-profit and the business sectors, primarily on a project basis. While away from salaried positions the past few years to give attention to personal matters, I have frequently been involved in community-based projects that enhanced my business skills and will make me more effective as an employee in the business sector.

For a simple job change—no career change, no market reentry:

After starting a career with [name of organization] *as a management trainee and rising up the career ladder there, I accepted an offer from* _____ *to work in their _____ division. I am now looking for a position with you because of their decision to leave [location]."*

For a career change:

After graduating from XYZ University with an engineering degree, I accepted a position with ABC Corporation to work for their _____ division. After five years of increased responsibility on a variety of projects, I was recruited for DEF, Inc. to be part of their new division specializing in _____. Now I am here because, as you may know, they have reconsidered their commitment to this area and have shut down that activity.

Practice your response until you are comfortable with an answer that takes about two minutes. After you give your answer, be quiet and wait for a response

☆ 6.2 Why are you leaving your current position? Why did you leave your last position?

Be consistent with your answer. Consider reasons you may have included in your cover letter, other conversations, on the application, and, if you were referred to the organization, in your conversation with the person who referred you. Additionally, if you are still employed or on speaking terms with your former employer, it is best **to have the same story for why you are no longer employed in case of reference checks.** It is a small world, and it is not a difficult task to corroborate your account.

What matters almost as much as the specific reason to this question is the tone and nonverbal gestures you use while giving your answer. You need to be comfortable and confident with the answer that you give, regardless of what you say. If you have been fired for whatever reason, speak cautiously. **Never lie, but remember you have control over what you say and how you say it.** Interviewers to whom you are telling your tale were not there, and they probably do not have a familiarity or understanding of the circumstances you are describing. You can certainly put a positive spin on any situation by describing how you learned from this development in your professional life.

If you are currently employed, the question might be phrased, ***"What is it about your current position that makes you feel that you would like to go elsewhere?"*** You can generate an answer with a positive spin due to:

❑ **Industry-wide changes.** *"New technology is making the organization's product obsolete." "Manufacturing is going off-shore."*

❑ **Organizational circumstances.** *"The organization is restructuring ... going out of business ... has been acquired/merged/spun off...."*

❏ **Geographical relocation.** *"The organization is leaving the area." "You/your spouse/your significant other requires a physical move and therefore new employment."*

❏ **Personal concerns.** *"Organizationally I have gone as far as I could. The person above me is just two years older and there is nowhere else for her to go at this time."* **Do not take the *"I've learned all that I could"* approach.** That contains a strong hint of *"I am only concerned about me and you need to keep me in a learning mode."* If that is what interviewers hear (whether that is an accurate reading of your comments or not), they may take that to mean that *"… if you hire me, you will have a problem because if you don't keep me in a learning opportunity, I will look elsewhere."*

❏ **Legal forms of harassment.** Mentioning forms of harassment other than sexual, while not illegal, serves to disclose to persons meeting with you that you have had problems with previous employers. Do they think you are worth the risk here? Harassment could include being threatened with termination for refusing to work overtime, bullying by a supervisor that seemed condoned by the organization, using harsh tones, a boisterous voice, or vulgar language as part of the ongoing terms and conditions of employment. Teasing or threats for whatever reason by supervisors or peers may all be valid reasons for your leaving your last employer.

6.3 Had you thought of leaving your current/past position before? If so, what held you there?

Good interviewers ask this question. They are attempting to learn your motivation and your ability to consider a course of action and then take it. There is a theory in the recruiting industry that is accepted as fact (and the few studies conducted to determine its accuracy tend to corroborate it). The theory states that anyone considering and accepting an offer who then takes a counteroffer from their current organization is out of their current organization within 18 months.

6.4 Are you looking for a permanent or temporary job?

This is a "gotcha" question. If you say the wrong thing, the interviewer knocks you out of the box. In the not too distant past, it used to be simple. There were those looking for permanent jobs and then a very small group who really preferred a temp job because of their unique personal or professional needs. Actors wanted temporary work so that they would be able to audition for parts whenever called upon to do so. Others who might have sought temp jobs included those between circumstances:

someone waiting for a spouse to be settled in a new location, a student waiting to return to school, and professional jockeys are some examples.

All that has changed. More people now seek temporary employment in order to allow them to pursue other interests that may be income-producing or not. Another group of people are working temporary jobs involuntarily—that is, because they are unable to secure regular full-time employment.

Notice too that the term "regular" was just used. More often than not, employers are avoiding the word "permanent" as a description for a type of job. They do it usually on the advice of counsel who feels that, by having a category of employee known as *permanent,* the employer may be inadvertently establishing a contractual obligation.

If you are interested only in temporary work and you say so, interviewers may dismiss your application because they need employees who are willing to stay. On the other hand, if the interviewer wants to hire employees on a contingency basis, and you say you want a permanent job, then the interviewer may lose interest in you.

If a permanent job is what you truly want, you do not lose by stating your preference directly. You are also able to show your astuteness if you add, *"Although I ideally would like a regular full-time job, I would be willing to be considered for a temporary position if that is all that is available because I would really like to work for this organization."* The tag-on at the end of your statement should grab the attention of the interviewer because you seem flexible and are interested in the organization. Consider your answer carefully beforehand because it offers your potential employer the opportunity to delay a "permanent" offer, because you are already conceding to a "look and see" approach.

6.5   *How do you feel about looking for another job?*

Take a positive, upbeat approach. *"Looking for another job is an opportunity."* Or, *"I don't have to look for another job. I do it so that I can continue to grow professionally."* What the interviewer hopes to hear is that you take charge of your own destiny. You are not looking because you have little or no choice. You need to demonstrate that you are in control and a go-getter.

✩ 6.6   *What has been the extent of your job search so far? How long have you been looking?*

The longer you have been looking for a job, the weaker you appear to interviewers because they will wonder why it is taking so long. Worse is the perception that, if no one is interested in hiring you, what are they doing spending time with you?

If you have been looking for a while and you want to admit it, then give it a positive spin. You have been looking for so long because you want to be careful about your next career move. You have had offers but nothing "rang the bell." If you take this route, be really ready to discuss the rejected offers because it is such an obvious opener that begs for the "next" question.

6.7 What career options do you have at this moment?

To share one or more alternatives here (in addition to the one you are discussing with the interviewer) is to risk the interviewer's perception either that you are not that interested in the position being discussed or that you are unfocused. There is an exception: Suppose you are beginning your career and meeting with a Personnel/Human Resource recruiter from an organization that offers several career options for entry-level college and graduate-level persons on a management track. In such a case, you can mention more than one option. For example, the person with a degree in finance and global management may consider either a domestic investment banking position or one in the international division. If that is shared with anyone in the organization, remember to stay consistent with that approach throughout the interview process in the organization. With luck, both groups may fight for you and the offer taken should not limit your going forward. Consider the recruitment meetings as network opportunities, and you should try to maintain those contacts as you move through the organization in your chosen career track.

When possible, open up the idea that you have many different facets.

> In my career in finance I have worked in both budgeting and cash flow management. Although I am coming from a management position in a budget department, I feel that managing your cash flow would be challenging and would be a job in which I could really add value to the organization.

6.8 What do you look for in a job?

Briefly put, describe a situation that shows you and the organization as linked. For example, "I am looking for a position where I can make a meaningful contribution continuously and grow professionally." You may also consider the best job you ever had (see question 6.11) to confirm your thoughts on this question before the meeting. Of course, having a positive correlation between this response and the job that the organization has open is an advantage.

6.9 Describe a major goal you have recently set for yourself.

Select a meaningful project that is either personal or professional in nature. "Complete my education" is one. "Find the right job" is another. The second is preferable because it brings the discussion back to the topic you are there to discuss—**a job for you in this specific organization.** To portray this as a major goal leaves no doubt about the fact one more time that you are very serious about a career and a job with the organization. This is a statement that does not hurt no matter how often you make it.

6.10 *Describe the best boss/supervisor that you ever had.*

When preparing yourself for this meeting and the job search, consider whom you most enjoyed working for as a boss. On a sheet of paper describe the qualities that that person possessed that affected his or her ability to be effective with you and the other members of the team. While you are at it, describe the qualities of the worst person you ever worked for. Compare your qualities lists for both and see what separates them. It is likely that your best boss's abilities to deal with people were linked with his or her ability to get the job done—namely to be sensitive to the needs and personalities of people.

When the question is asked at your meeting, you are then ready to briefly describe the situation and speak genuinely about the boss. If you have not thought about it before the meeting, you have to pause while you reflect on who your best boss was and then consider what to say before saying it. This is a tough task given the circumstances and pressures of a job interview. Again, if the qualities and type of management style mirror that which you feel the organization aspires to attract, you have scored major points.

6.11 *Describe the best job you ever had.*

By preparing for this question ahead of time, you avoid the need to consider the question on the spot, do a quick sort to find the job, and then scramble mentally to put a coherent statement together. This question may not be dissimilar from the previous question *"What do you look for in a job?"* because, by considering the best job you ever had, you probably identify specifics that help you decide what you are looking for in a job. *Do not make your "best" job too dissimilar from the one you are being considered for.*

☆ 6.12 *How do you feel about your career progress to date?*

When defining career objectives and evaluating your progress to date in the confines of a very private environment, you should deal frankly with this question. Regardless of the answer that you share and the answer that perhaps you keep to yourself at this interviewing session, demonstrate satisfaction to a point, and that point is the reason for deciding to move on in this direction now.

6.13   *How do you define success?*

This is another personal query that should be considered before the meeting, not so much for the interviewer's sake as for your own. In the meeting however, realize that the person asking the question is asking it in an organizational—not a career counseling—context. You may consider **linking recognition to meaningful contribution** as an answer: *"I define success as being able to financially provide for my family while performing work that is tied to the success of the organization that employs me."*

6.14   *What personal characteristics do you think will be needed to be a success in this position?*

From the work you have already completed as part of your Personal Worksheet and On the Job EQ, this should not be a difficult question to address at the interview. Review the list thoroughly before the meeting because you want to be sure you do not take this topic for granted. Persistence, loyalty, strong work ethic, strong communication skills, results orientation, team player, insatiable curiosity—these are among the characteristics that may be included. Be ready to provide instances where you put to use any of the characteristics mentioned for the possibility of follow-up questions.

Review your On the Job EQ list. Persistence, loyalty, strong work ethic, strong communication skills, results orientation, team player, insatiable curiosity (as already mentioned) are all admirable qualities that are accepted in any work environment and certainly could be used for starters.

6.15   *If you could, what would you change about this position?*

Beware of interviewers who raise this question. Either they are tapping your brain to get some free consulting or want to see if you are already changing things before the job is even offered. Don't be tempted. Unless something is truly glaring, you would be best advised to say, *"Until I am actually in the position and see what works and what doesn't, I would be hard pressed to make any recommendations."*

☆ 6.16   *What do you like the most about this position? What do you like the least about this position?*

This question usually has two parts, which come one at a time. The setup comes with asking what you like best first because it is the easier of the two. (If you cannot think of any positives, why are you still there?) To answer what you like the most, identify two or three major job elements or characteristics that really are the essence of the job:

I like the amount of time that will be devoted to outside clients.

I particularly like the problem solving elements of the position.

The team that I would work with looks terrific.

When being positioned to identify the least attractive aspects of the position, try to avoid the question by saying, *"I can't think of anything that I dislike about the position."* Or, *"It sounds just like what I had hoped it would be."* Appear confident and knowledgeable about the position. Then try to share something that the interviewer has already mentioned about it so that you are an empathizing, perceptive, and good listener. Or come up with an obvious, minor drawback:

The only thing that will make the position a difficult one is the two-block distance between the department's location and the group it is expected to serve.

6.17 Do you prefer delegation or "hands-on" control?

This is a good question because there is **no right or wrong answer.** The interviewer is trying to **determine the "fit" of your approach** to work with the environment. If you prefer delegation, you need to build a mutual feeling of trust in your subordinates. "Hands-on" control demands a different approach by you and by each subordinate. This question should be directly and openly answered because, if the situation requires a real delegating manager and you happen to be real "hands-on," the fit is not a good one unless you are really flexible. Even then, the chances are that, even if you are hired, when the pressure mounts, you will revert to your old management style—and that could spell disaster.

6.18 What kind of people do you like to work with? What do you feel is the easiest type of person to deal with? The most difficult?

These three relationship questions seek to determine what makes for an easy personal interaction for you. Do you prefer the direct, hands-on approach, or do you look instead for the person who just gives you enormous autonomy? To be prepared for any of these questions, determine whom:

❏ You are best able to deal with.

❏ You have had to deal with organizationally, and are best to work for and with.

❏ You have had the greatest difficulty working with.

To take a comprehensive approach and to be sure you are identifying every possible type of person you have had to interact with at work, think up, down, and at the same level. If you are hit with any of these questions, be prepared to answer all three questions.

"Who is the most difficult person to work with?" is not as easy to deal with as the other two questions. But do not become worried or defensive because this is really a gift question. Try to identify annoying characteristics that are typically abhorred:

The person who refuses to stay when asked to help to solve a problem.
Fellow workers who work at a pace that just barely keeps them employed.
Someone who tries to avoid responsibility for deadlines.

If you agree that one or more of these types are the worst, then you have your answer.

6.19 What are your long-range goals?

Be practical and realistic. Demonstrate that you are a person with a future orientation.

I would like to continue over the long term to make ongoing contributions to the organization's success while growing professionally.

☆ 6.20 What are your strong points?
What are your weak points?

Take this opportunity to share with the interviewer your strong points, including qualities that are relevant for the position at hand and also important to you. Loyalty, a strong work ethic, good interpersonal and communications skills, a project and results orientation are all personal characteristics that interviewers love to hear. Be prepared to give situations that exemplify one or more of your personal characteristics.

These questions often travel on the heels of each other. Do not be as open with your weaknesses as with your strong points. Try to identify qualities (or their lack) that are not so relevant to the position being discussed.

I must admit I am a workaholic.
I am impatient with others who display no sense of urgency.

Or damn yourself with faint praise:

I always try to come in ahead of deadlines.

6.21 *What is your greatest accomplishment?*

If possible, keep your answer focused on work. *"To convince management to proceed with this multimillion dollar project—and make it work,"* is a grand answer if you have such a situation to draw upon. Most of us, though, do not have that luxury and must select more mundane and perhaps boring subjects instead. A careful review of your past experiences should provide the preparation necessary to field this question in a most effective manner.

If you cannot stick with a work-related situation, identify a situation that is of interest to the interviewer. Practice being a good storyteller. People love brief, interesting stories. Restoration of a house, completing college, or raising a family would certainly all qualify. The more you are able to confine the discussion to work-related issues, however, the more interviewers see information that they consider strong evidence of a person who gets things done.

6.22 *If I spoke to your current/former boss, what would he or she say are your greatest strengths/ your greatest weaknesses?*

These questions may be a sign of an inexperienced interviewer or an ineffective or poor listener, who is asking formula questions and not paying attention to answers. Go back to your earlier answers on personal strengths and highlight a few associated with your most recent position. As to weaknesses, you can't say, *"My boss would say that he/she has a difficult time identifying any weaknesses in my current position."* If you do, you have avoided the question successfully but that "victory" also means that interviewers are repulsed or frustrated in their attempt to get a discussion going. Not a move without consequences. Instead your interviewer may ponder whether your evasiveness is a pattern (and determine you are not someone the organization should pursue further). You could point out something that you learned or overcame that used to be a weakness.

> *I used to be a worker who always wanted to complete every project perfectly. I have learned to determine a quality standard and be realistic about its importance in the context of the variety of tasks and projects I am responsible for.*

☆ 6.23 *What do you think of your current/former boss?*

In preparation for this answer, remember the survey mentioned in Chap. 3 that found that about 80 percent of all of the survey's outplacement clients reported that they felt the reason they had lost their jobs was because of their relationship with their bosses.

Even though the question has been raised, **caution, not candor, is the rule.** Keep focused on the reason for the question: The interviewer needs to determine whether you are appropriate and suitable for this organization and whether they have a suitable position with a suitable supervisor for you. *This is a direct assessment question to determine if there is a fit between you and the situation they are considering you for.* Your choice of words when discussing your boss gives the interviewer a chance to assess your ability and under what conditions of leadership you can function most effectively. Be brief and specific. It is important that you begin with positives. No matter how bad you (and perhaps countless others) perceived the person to be, this is not the time to disclose your strong negative feelings.

At the same time do not overpraise. By giving an assessment that is weighted toward the positive but balanced, you are demonstrating to the interviewer the depth you have in assessing the performance of others and your ability to work with others by playing to strengths and supporting weaknesses.

A sample answer then will go like this:

> *I respected my boss because she had a tough job due to all the changes going on organizationally and in the marketplace—yet she was able to get the work done. In spite of all this, she was effective because she balanced the needs of the team with those demanded by her own boss so that she absorbed a lot of the pressure herself and her team understood what she was doing. At times she had difficulty balancing these various needs and it would occasionally show because she would cut corners and quality would suffer.*

Let us consider a worst-case boss. For a truly terrible boss for whom you had no respect and who was miserable as a person, you might consider:

> *My boss was one of the most challenging persons I have had the opportunity to work for anywhere in my career so far. He had a lot going on personally that made his working situation a particularly difficult one. Because of the internal situation, he seemed driven by the need to concentrate on the task aspects of his responsibilities and as a result the "people needs" were given less than the needed attention. We had a lot of company-induced turnover as a result that led to more challenges for him and added to the stress of the situation for him.*

6.24 What features did you like the least/the most about your current/last position?

This is a great question for both you and the interviewer. For you, it is great (provided you are prepared) because it affords you the opportunity to demonstrate how you perceive work. Just be careful to stay focused and brief. Go back to the exercise in Chap. 4, Job History Worksheet and see what items you can highlight. Obviously, *the aspects you like least are what have brought you to this interview and the features you like best are those that have kept you at that job up to now.* Select features on your least-liked list that are probably not at the new organization (or ones that they would not espouse), while the ones you selected as those you liked coincidentally are also part of the new position!

☆ 6.25 *In your current/last position, state your five most significant accomplishments?*

This question raises the issue of your most recent job in a different but still very open-ended way. It should be a question that you welcome and relish because it is a real opportunity for you to discuss openly what you accomplished on your assignment. For details, you can refer to your Experience Worksheet. Consider the question a compliment to you because the person raising the question is most probably a serious, well trained interviewer. This may appear to be an obvious question, but it is not that frequently asked.

Your answer, in tone as well as in content, should be consistent with all of your bearing and presentation until now. This answer should confirm what had been discussed previously and, if there is any revelation, then this is your opportunity to confirm that the interviewer should not be surprised.

6.26 *What will you do if this position is not offered to you?*

This is a silly question but treat it seriously if asked. Act disappointed but professional.

> *Since the interview seems to be going smoothly and my qualifications appear to satisfy the job requirements, I would be curious as to what area of inquiry was not satisfactory. Since I am very impressed with this organization, I would ask for some feedback and whether I could be considered for other similar positions in the future.*

6.27 *Where do you hope to be professionally in five years?*

This is one of those standard questions that someone thought up years ago and for some reason it has continued to grow in popularity. It is not a bad question because it is open-ended with a time line. The applicant is expected to provide a realistic answer that portrays neither a lust for power (*"I want to be your boss"*) nor a lack of focus and ambition (*"I want to be right where I am, or win the lottery and spend the rest of my life watching*

TV"). Instead, the candidate is expected to show bridled ambition (except in a few organizations that want to see a "killer" attitude):

> *I hope to continue to be with this organization in a position of increased responsibility where I will be able to continue my professional growth while making an ongoing corporate contribution to the organization's continued success.*

6.28 Would you consider volunteering at our organization?

Watch out for this one. First of all, only not-for-profits are legally allowed to take volunteers. There is the minimum wage law to consider. I mention this not to cause a conflict with the organization raising the question but to make sure that you consider the offer in light of your own interest. These days some employers in the private sector in several industries accept "interns" for unpaid positions, and there are takers at that price. Consider whether it enhances your value to a potential employer to accept a nonpaying job in the hope of getting a paying one later. Be careful because frequently a perception goes with your salary level, bluntly stated as, *"You get what you pay for."*

Keep in mind also that the time you spend as a volunteer is time not spent looking for a job. There is a trade-off of your time and attendant costs in working for "free" with the ability of getting your foot in the door and receiving on-the-job training. This tactic might be more valuable when considering a career change or entry-level positions. To show interest in the organization but discourage your being thought of as free labor, try saying:

> *I would jump at the chance to be part of your organization, but unfortunately my financial situation precludes my foregoing a salary at this point.*

6.29 Would you like to have your [prospective] supervisor's job?

Be diplomatic. *"I need to concentrate on the position I am being considered for at this time. That will be more than enough to occupy my efforts for quite a while to come."*

6.30 Are you creative?

Every job demands more or less creativity. If you are a copy writer in an ad agency, you are required to take blank pieces of paper and type out thoughts that not only are creative but that also reflect the product or service which you are being paid to advertise. If you are looking to be a supervisor in a bookkeeping department, creativity is not highly valued. A creative person, dealing with debits and credits and journal entries, may not be a valid match for the position. **Determine the kinds and level of creativity that are inherent in the open position, and offer examples from your experience that complement them.**

⭐ *6.31   How would you describe your own personality?*

Review the first section of the Personal Worksheet that you completed earlier to choose the adjectives that are "you." Do not be afraid to use a dictionary or thesaurus to be absolutely certain about various shades of meaning.

> *Gregarious* (Watch for sexist biases.)
> *Attention to detail*
> *Work oriented*
> *Task driven*
> *Stickler for time*
> *Focused*
> *Attentive*
> *Sensitive*
> *Empathetic*
> *Aggressive/assertive*
> *Self-motivated*
> *High energy*
> *Self-starter*
> *Parsimonious*
> *Loyal*
> *Punctual*
> *Control-oriented*
> *Team player*
> *Questioning*

There is no reason to do this alone. Ask friends, family, and business associates what words could be used to describe you. In many cases, friends are delighted to help with your job search in any capacity. *Ask yourself what kind of personality is needed to fill the position and cite your characteristics that support your candidacy.*

⭐ *6.32   May I have your business card?*

If you have portrayed yourself as a consultant, this could be a pop quiz. *The business card is used as an essential tool, and the quality of the card (texture, logo, print) are all a part of the statement that you are making.* Even if you are not consulting, it is a good idea to have a card and offer it whether or not the question is asked. What is perfectly polite and correct is to ask for a card at the end of the meeting because one has yet to be offered. When you offer one of yours in exchange for theirs, you are reciprocating—a warm, friendly, and totally professional gesture. Don't do as one job applicant did and give the interviewer a business card identifying herself as a member of an occult group specializing in witchcraft.

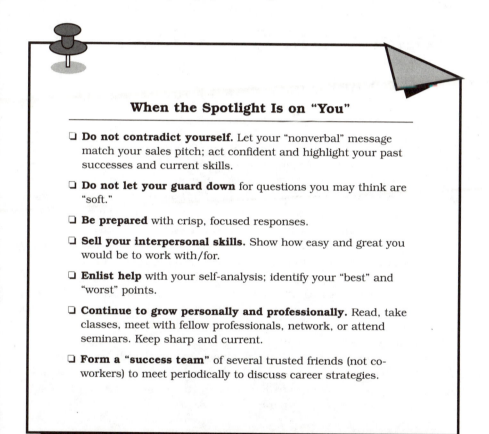

When the Spotlight Is on "You"

❏ **Do not contradict yourself.** Let your "nonverbal" message match your sales pitch; act confident and highlight your past successes and current skills.

❏ **Do not let your guard down** for questions you may think are "soft."

❏ **Be prepared** with crisp, focused responses.

❏ **Sell your interpersonal skills.** Show how easy and great you would be to work with/for.

❏ **Enlist help** with your self-analysis; identify your "best" and "worst" points.

❏ **Continue to grow personally and professionally.** Read, take classes, meet with fellow professionals, network, or attend seminars. Keep sharp and current.

❏ **Form a "success team"** of several trusted friends (not co-workers) to meet periodically to discuss career strategies.

7

Educational Questions

What Do You Know?

A recent magazine article stated that the *single most important career law* is **to constantly reinvent yourself and your career.** In this competitive market, it is not the "know it all" who attracts the best offers but the individual who is constantly learning. Learning in classrooms, learning on the job, and life experience all point favorably toward job applicants who can grow with the organization and be dynamic in their positions.

Interviewers are interested in your "professional" education: **what do you know about the industry, their organization, the position, and your relationship to the future of their organization?** They seek to determine how professionally skilled and developed you are. How do you learn? Where are you intellectually? How much research have you done into their business? How astute are you?

If you go into an interview thinking that the questions that may be asked will be concentrated solely on subject matter directly related to the jobs that you have had and the schools you have attended, you will be unprepared for the following questions, which may very well be included during the course of your meeting.

The "Knowledge Worker" and the Postindustrial Era

The "knowledge worker" as a concept is becoming ever more widely accepted, in organizational use, as an accurate portrayal of what the postindustrial era corporation requires. With that growing acceptance of the concept, the worker with "knowledge skills" is becoming increasingly in demand in the workplace.

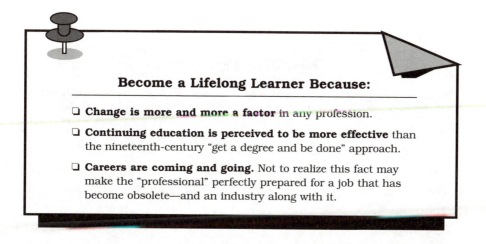

Become a Lifelong Learner Because:

❑ **Change is more and more a factor** in any profession.

❑ **Continuing education is perceived to be more effective** than the nineteenth-century "get a degree and be done" approach.

❑ **Careers are coming and going.** Not to realize this fact may make the "professional" perfectly prepared for a job that has become obsolete—and an industry along with it.

To review all that you do "know" and your educational history, complete the Education Worksheet (page 80). Do not neglect to list any on-the-job training, seminars or workshops you may have attended, or classes that you may be currently taking or enrolled in. Which of these you disclose as being relevant to the job opening is certainly under your control.

Knowledge, of course, is not limited to instructional situations; review again the third section (What I Know) of the Personal Worksheet to remind yourself of "hidden" skills. Again, if you are applying for a job as an administrative assistant, you may not wish to disclose your steno skills. *Consider what skills or types of knowledge are necessary for this position (and for future advancement)* and list these on the On the Job IQ form (page 81). To be certain you have them in your repertoire write next to each skill or knowledge how you came by it or where you acquired it. For example, you may have a knowledge of Quicken accounting software because you use it for your personal checking records or you may be able to speak and write Spanish due to a stint in the military. Of particular importance is your honesty in rating the level of proficiency you can offer the organization.

☆ 7.1 *How much would it take to get you?*
What do you feel this position should pay?

Depending on when in the interview process either of these questions is raised, it establishes the level of seriousness. If after three intensive interviews, the question *"How much would it take to get you?"* is raised, it may mean that an offer is about to be negotiated. If, on the other hand, interviewers ask *"What do you feel this position should pay?"* as part of the first interview, they may very well be trying to get applicants to knock themselves out of contention with the wrong answer. Another reason may be

Education Worksheet

Provide details for each school or academic experience listed on your resume, starting with the current or most recent.

Name of school: _____

Address: _____

Telephone number: _____

Date started: _____

Major courses of study: _____

Degree received (or anticipated): _____

Date graduated (or expected): _____

Academic awards/honors: _____

Courses that relate to job search: _____

_____

How do these courses relate to the position sought? _____

_____

Why did you choose this school? _____

_____

Why did you choose this course of study? _____

_____

If a recent graduate, name and telephone number of academic reference:

_____

_____

Graduate school? Thesis/dissertation subject: _____

_____

Future academic plans: _____

_____

Seminars/workshops (dates, location/sponsor, and subject): _____

_____

_____

_____

On the Job IQ

Organization: _____

Position: _____

Rate your level of proficiency: 1 = beginner   2 = experienced   3 = expert

Skills/knowledge needed for this position	Specific example of when/where you acquired skill/knowledge:	Level

that the interviewer has not determined the price and is using you to determine the amount.

If the question is raised early, such as anytime in the first interview, you may respond by saying, *"I really do not have enough details for the position in question to determine an amount."* If the question is asked later, that response sounds weak. If by then you are not clear about the duties and responsibilities of the position and how the position is pegged in the organization, *you* may be perceived as weak and a poor listener to boot.

If you must answer, you can ask first about similar jobs (but *not* amounts at this point) in the organization. Try using a question such as, *"What other jobs are similar to this one in the organization?"* If provided with information, ask the salary range for those positions.

Continue by saying what you may feel is obvious, *"Is there any additional consideration that would require you to pay at a different level for this position?"* Notice that you still try to avoid mentioning a specific dollar amount.

If the answer is negative, then you may say without additional information and without knowing the details of the benefits and other forms of compensation (bonus and incentive payments, last and next anticipated increase dates), it is difficult to provide a number worthy of consideration.

If still pressed, consider giving a range of numbers. An example is, *"... between $33,000 and $38,000 if the assumptions I am making about other factors are accurate."* Have some estimate in mind before showing up for the meeting.

Sometimes you get the interview without the benefit of any opportunity (for example, want ads or recruiters) to determine the price for the position, or you have the interview but you are not sure what position, if any, will be discussed. In such cases, try to find out at the first opportunity, without appearing mercenary. By asking, you negate any opportunity for interviewers to ask the same question (unless they forget that they told you, and that doesn't that make you seem astute).

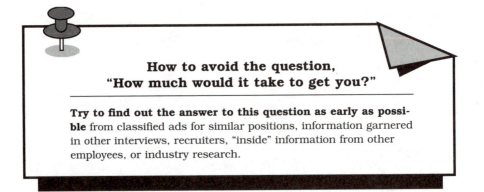

How to avoid the question, "How much would it take to get you?"

Try to find out the answer to this question as early as possible from classified ads for similar positions, information garnered in other interviews, recruiters, "inside" information from other employees, or industry research.

You need to be extremely careful because, if you ask too early what the position pays, the interviewer may determine that you are too interested in money and therefore not a candidate worthy of further consideration.

It is fair that you be informed fairly early in the process of the range for the position because it is *mutually beneficial to both parties to determine whether there is a basis for further discussion.* The higher up you are on the pay scale and the higher your desired salary level, the more this is true. The worst thing for any recruiter to do is to go to the offer stage—to discover that the organization is offering only $19,000 for the position when your last salary, as indicated on your completed employment application, was $42,500 for the same type of position.

7.2 *If you could start your career over again, what would you do differently?*

Beware of this "road not taken" question. You must be careful not to sound wistful. Remember that you are not dealing with a therapist but a job interviewer. Mention if you cannot think of anything that, *"I am satisfied with my career and the direction it has taken."* Then, if you do think of anything you may have done differently, try to consider something that would have made your arrival at your current point swifter: *"I only wish that I had applied to this organization when I was starting."*

☆ 7.3 *If you could choose any organization, where would you go?*

This is an opportunity for you to demonstrate the depth of your knowledge and scope of your interest. Do not overwhelm. State simply, *"This is the kind of organization I am looking for because...."*

☆ 7.4 *What do you know about the position for which you are applying?*

This is a good opportunity to clear the air. If you have a lot of information about the position, speak confidently and briefly. If you have little or no information, say so. *Rule of thumb: A little information is a better response than none.* If you have no information about the position, the burden is on you to have a reason for applying for a position about which you know nothing—not an impossible situation, but usually somewhat odd. This is a question you should ask yourself regularly as you go through the selection process, and salient facts should be marked on your Organization Fact Sheet.

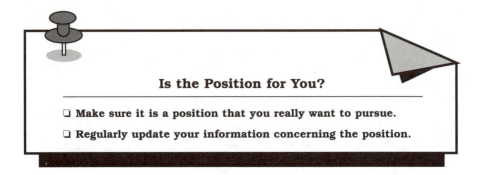

Is the Position for You?

❏ **Make sure it is a position that you really want to pursue.**

❏ **Regularly update your information concerning the position.**

Do not forget that the purpose of the interview is to share information; do not be afraid to get additional information about the position if you need to.

☆ 7.5 *What is your overall impression of this position/organization?*

Based on your professional knowledge and instincts, you should be prepared for this question—whether the question is asked during the interview—because you should have asked if of yourself. If subtitles were provided for these questions, they would be, *"Why do you want this job?"* and *"Why do you want to work here?"* Provide the interviewer with an answer that is not as frank or lengthy as the answer you have come up with in discussions with yourself. This is an opportunity to show the depth of your knowledge and the reach of your contacts by *sharing briefly what you have learned about the organization from the interview process and from all the information you have gathered about the organization and the position.*

☆ 7.6 *What is the most recent skill you learned? What was the newest thing that you learned how to do?*

The answer is the essence of this chapter: **Portray yourself as an interested, active, lifelong learner.** Try to avoid putting a time frame on your answer (unless you took a workshop just the other day). This question is a prime example of why it is important to prepare and to complete the various worksheets highlighting your work and education history.

7.7 *How do you learn? What is your learning style (hands-on, research, by example)?*

This nice question gives you the opportunity to talk about yourself without any really right or wrong implications. With the question, interviewers are not, as it might seem, making a notation so that, if you are offered the job, you will be given training tailored to your most effective learning style. No, the question seeks to see if you are able to learn quickly and be ready to perform immediately after the training program, regardless of its brevity. This is, in short, not the place to say, *"I really prefer to study all facets of an issue and become an expert before performing any related activity."* The only thing that has not been added is, *"... and if that takes years...."* Interviewers will not remember the phrase was not included because it will seem as though it had been.

It is best to present an action-oriented format that underscores that the best way to learn is when you get to perform on the job immediately after any training is completed. If there is opportunity to practice during the learning session, so much the better.

The last element to mention, but not demand, is feedback. You like occasional feedback to ensure that you are putting into action correctly what you have been trained to do. Don't emphasize constant or regular feedback because then the interviewers see that you require constant attention—a problem!

⭐ 7.8 *How do you keep informed professionally?*

The question *assumes that you do keep informed professionally* and that you consider yourself a professional. What do you read on a daily basis? Weekly? Biweekly? Monthly? Quarterly? Depending on your field, a variety of materials are published on all these schedules. The "quarterlies" usually contain lengthy articles that provide serious, in-depth treatment of a topic. Notice the first activity mentioned in response to the question is "read." With the proliferation of the television into every area of our lives, the TV frequently replaces print media in the development of our

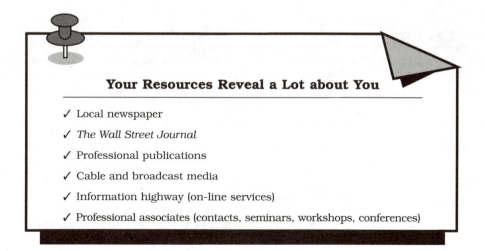

Your Resources Reveal a Lot about You

✓ Local newspaper

✓ *The Wall Street Journal*

✓ Professional publications

✓ Cable and broadcast media

✓ Information highway (on-line services)

✓ Professional associates (contacts, seminars, workshops, conferences)

intellectual skills, both personally and professionally. The more you grow in your profession, the more you are expected to pursue sources of information that provide increasingly sophisticated data to regularly give breadth and depth to your knowledge base.

☆ 7.9 What have you learned from the jobs that you have held?

This is an opportunity for you to *summarize your experience from a learning perspective.* Review your Experience Worksheet (page 93) to see what skills and accomplishments developed from job to job. Mention both the task aspects of work as well as the people relationships, saying directly that your most important relationship is to your boss or immediate supervisor. Try to include the terms "respect" and "loyalty" when speaking in an organizational context and discussing its products and/or services. Comment about the value you bring to any job. A sample answer follows:

> *I have learned to define what value I add to the organization to ensure that what I am being compensated is worth that and more to the organization. I know that process is a consideration, but results and output are most important. If the organization is going to be competitive, the employees need a customer perspective and to have that, they need to work effectively together. Last, the organization that I work for requires my respect and loyalty.*

7.10 Do you feel that you have top management potential?

Be realistic about your abilities, especially the higher you rise professionally. A way to avoid a right or wrong answer is to qualify your answer with the comment *"… depending on the organization."*

7.11 Why did you go to law school/business school/college?

Any question that includes the word "why" sets an adult-child tone that is the antithesis of workplace relationships. Even though there may be a tendency to give a "smart" answer or perhaps a humorous one, remember the reason for meeting with the interviewer. Be ready with a firm, serious answer that demonstrates that, even as a youth with little experience, you were sure about what you wanted to do with the rest of your life.

> *The reason for going to college was to develop myself intellectually and to prepare for life ahead by taking the disciplines necessary to develop my mind. I knew then that _____ skills would always be necessary and a(n) _____ education would develop those skills in an organized, deliberate way.*

The reason for graduate-level education may include pursuing a discipline that would enhance your abilities to deal effectively in the marketplace with focused studies and a particular perspective (law, business, engineering). If you are not practicing the field that you studied, mention that it was not your intention to pursue a profession in that field.

> *Although I did get a law degree, it was not to practice as an attorney. I felt that a legal background combined with my business degree would uniquely prepare me to assume a position in an international organization.*

If you have a solid reason for a change in profession, state it succinctly.

7.12   Why did you attend that particular school/college?

Do not be frivolous or cute, regardless of the degree of temptation. Interviewers possibly have positive or negative feelings about the school and may even have gone there themselves—or a close family member might have. Practice your answer before the meeting. It is not necessary to give the real answer. **Remember that you are in control of what you wish to disclose and that your reason for the meeting is to continue the interview process and other selection steps so that a job offer will be given to you.**

For now give the reason that makes the most sense to you and that makes you appear a promising candidate in the interviewer's eyes.

> *I saw several articles written by faculty members and was impressed with their command of the subject.*
>
> *In addition to having a wide range of business courses, the timing of the classes allowed me to work part-time in the field I was studying.*

7.13   What made you choose to become a lawyer/banker/ secretary/engineer?

Avoid all temptations to be cute even though the question has little bearing on the individual you are now. Before the meeting, go through an exercise to see if you can recall the motivation you had to become a lawyer, engineer, etc. During the process, determine also why you chose not to go into other fields. Parents and other family members are frequently role models for our professional choices.

The important thing about this question is to demonstrate with your answer that *you were always serious about your career* and that your seriousness has carried forward to this day, so that interviewers feel they are dealing with a prospective employee with a solid history of professional growth and development.

⭐ 7.14   *What is our business? What do you know about our organization?*

If you are unprepared for this one, you should not be sitting in this meeting in the first place. Even for courtesy interviews, **be prepared** by finding out whatever you can about the organization with whom you will be meeting.

Consider the question from a selfish point of view:

❏ **Why is this organization for you?**

❏ **What makes you take the time to meet with them rather than the practically millions of others?**

❏ **What value can you offer to this organization?**

You owe it to yourself to learn as much as you can about any organization that you intend to visit. What you choose to share, however, really takes fine judgment on your part. If you uncover dirt, you do not want to mention it here. If meeting with a television company, now is not the time, for example, to speak about the appalling lack of quality children's programming.

Provide a concise overview of your findings that shows you are aware of what the organization does and the size of its operations. *"XYZ bank is a tri-state bank committed to the retail sector. It has 42 branches and plans to open seven more in the next two years."* If you show some knowledge about the organization, especially if the information is not that easy to obtain, you make a good impression. Be careful not to overwhelm because the situation may become uncomfortable if you share something the interviewer was unaware of.

⭐ 7.15   *What do you think our business' biggest problem is? What do you feel is our biggest advantage over our competition?*

Here is an opportunity to show not only that you did your homework in preparing for this meeting but that you have great professional bearing and an in-depth knowledge of the industry and its other key players. Again, do not overwhelm. **Do not show up interviewers by discussing a topic in more detail than they are equipped to handle.** Also, as far as problems are concerned, try to **avoid controversy.** Your interviewer does not know that you are aware of the indictments against the corporation's top three officers for price fixing unless you share it. (Remember our discussion in Chap. 3 on disclosure.) Instead, select a product-related problem like the rising cost of newsprint if you happen to be meeting with a print media organization.

> *Organization _____ appears to have excellent demographic information. Your programs always seem to be topical and on the cutting edge while the other networks are merely following up on the newest trends.*

☆ 7.16 *What important trends do you see in our industry?*

This is a serious question that requires focus and preparation. It demands proof that you have done your homework. You are meeting with the interviewer not only because you need a job but also, regardless of your circumstances, because *you have done your research* and *you have real reasons for wanting to join this organization* and be a part of this specific industry. To prepare to answer this question you need to be able to speak knowledgeably about:

1. The industry.

2. What issues relate to the industry.

3. How the organization perceives its effectiveness in dealing with the trends that the industry faces.

All this is not something that takes a lifetime to learn but something that requires a willingness to do research as part of the preparation for any meeting for a job. Go to the Organization Fact Sheet and file to determine if you have enough information to speak intelligently on the industry. Of particular importance is how you can see yourself making a positive difference to the organization in the future:

> *Clearly the biggest trend is the move to on-line communication. Interactive "magazines" may be the wave of the future and, with my journalist background combined with my recent introduction to JAVA, I am really excited about how I will help change the future of the publishing industry.*

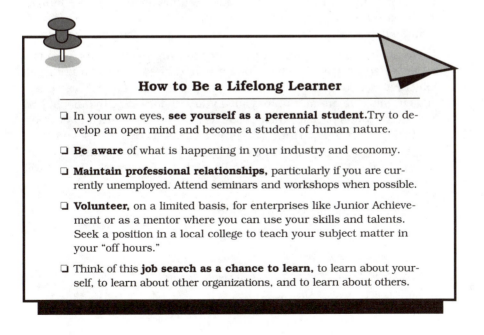

How to Be a Lifelong Learner

❏ In your own eyes, **see yourself as a perennial student.** Try to develop an open mind and become a student of human nature.

❏ **Be aware** of what is happening in your industry and economy.

❏ **Maintain professional relationships,** particularly if you are currently unemployed. Attend seminars and workshops when possible.

❏ **Volunteer,** on a limited basis, for enterprises like Junior Achievement or as a mentor where you can use your skills and talents. Seek a position in a local college to teach your subject matter in your "off hours."

❏ Think of this **job search as a chance to learn,** to learn about yourself, to learn about other organizations, and to learn about others.

8

Experience Questions

What Have You Done?

Experience questions are the most important to deal with for three reasons:

1. **Experience questions force applicants to review what has previously occurred in their professional lives.** This exercise provides an opportunity for recall and analysis, something that all people who are serious about their work should do periodically. If you do not go through this exercise, then a lot of what you have done in the past is lost and mistakes could possibly be repeated because you forget the situation and most importantly the outcome.

2. These questions and the behavioral questions should be **the benchmark on which the decision to continue the interview process,** and ultimately the hire/don't hire decision is made by the interviewer.

3. These questions are a **great opportunity for you to shine,** for who is a better expert on yourself than you? It would be folly for you not to be fully prepared for questions regarding your past experience. When questions in this area are raised, they give you a chance to sell yourself. Just as manufacturers package their products in attractive boxes and develop marketing campaigns to tout their products' latest advantages, you must create a sales campaign for yourself. What are your best points? How can you add value to the organization? To retain interviewers' interest, you must present a positive image from the first moment you meet them.

Experience questions take various forms:

Describe your last job.
Tell me about your last boss.
What kind of an environment do you do your best work in?
What was your biggest mistake?

Putting Your Best Foot Forward

The following traits are the personal characteristics to be displayed throughout every interview, but especially in responses to questions regarding one's experience.

❑ **Preparation:** You are taking the interview process seriously.

❑ **Enthusiasm:** You are excited by the work you have already done and look forward to the future.

❑ **Communication effectiveness:** You are able to speak cogently and appear to be a savvy person who can discuss work in an interesting and intelligent manner.

❑ **Focus:** The main topic of an interview should center around your professional experience.

❑ **Subject matter expert:** You are *the* expert on what you have been doing at work.

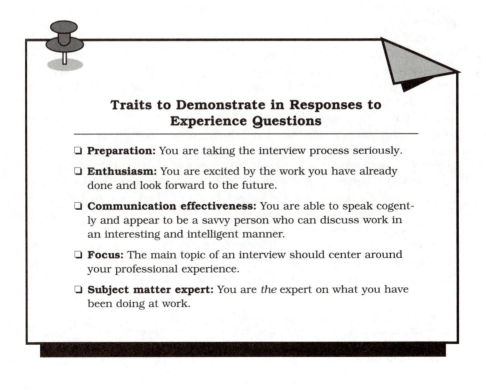

Traits to Demonstrate in Responses to Experience Questions

❑ **Preparation:** You are taking the interview process seriously.

❑ **Enthusiasm:** You are excited by the work you have already done and look forward to the future.

❑ **Communication effectiveness:** You are able to speak cogently and appear to be a savvy person who can discuss work in an interesting and intelligent manner.

❑ **Focus:** The main topic of an interview should center around your professional experience.

❑ **Subject matter expert:** You are *the* expert on what you have been doing at work.

Preinterview Preparation

Interviewers seek insights and details of your professional experiences with people and relationships with superiors and subordinates, information regarding your experiences with projects and tasks (both positive and negative), and other information regarding your work experience.

Preinterview preparation is time well spent because it offers an opportunity to consider your job from another (and frequently missed) vantage point. *Three hours of preparation, including research on the organization and the industry, appears to be a reasonable time to invest for each interview.* A first step is to take a copy of your most recent resume and come up with all the details and salient points of your professional history that are not included in the resume itself but that all should be literally "at the tip of your tongue" for your interview. Using the Experience Worksheet (page 93), provide all the details (who, what, when, where, and why) for your current or most recent job and for all the jobs listed on your resume. Do not omit any military service or volunteer experience.

Continue your preparation for these questions by looking at "critical incidents" that were a part of your job for the past three months or the last three months that you were there, if you have been out awhile. The reason for taking the last three months is that, by considering the most recent experience, this first exercise makes it easier to recall earlier incidents (six months, a year).

Critical incidents are those that are out of the customary and ordinary process of doing business under usual or ordinary circumstances. It should be the exciting part of any job because it represents a challenge. The situations may require high risk but also offer greater reward. Use the Critical Incidents Worksheet (page 94) to perform this exercise. Do not confine your review to only those incidents where things were all in your favor, but include times when problems ensued or your work was criticized. What did you learn from these "mistakes"?

You may be familiar with the Nordstrom's story about the clerk who has become a legend for Nordstrom's. When a customer returned tires and demanded a refund, the clerk gave the refund and took the tires back. So far no big deal, right? What begins to make the situation a "critical incident" is that Nordstrom's does not sell tires, and this is where the unusual occurs both in terms of the employee and the organization. There are organizations who would fire a clerk for such an action. At Nordstrom's they decided to praise it and make this "critical incident" a part of their organizational culture because they want their employees to know:

> To the customer (or potential customer, as in this case), service and satisfaction are primary objectives and employees have the authority to exercise discretion when called upon by circumstances and will not be punished for it.

Experience Worksheet

Provide details for each job listed on your resume, starting with the current or most recent job.

Employer: _____

Address: _____

Telephone number: _____

Supervisor's name: _____

Supervisor's telephone number: _____

Date started: _____   Last day of work: _____

Starting salary: _____   Current/ending salary: _____

Starting position: _____   Current/ending position: _____

Starting title: _____   Current/ending title: _____

How did you get this job? _____

_____

Describe most recent duties: _____

Describe your work group: _____

On what basis was your work evaluated? _____

Who evaluated your work? _____   How often? _____

What evaluation did you last receive? _____

How many hours did you usually work each week? _____

Overtime? _____   How often? _____   Why? _____

What did you like best about this job? _____

_____

... the least? _____

_____

What are your greatest accomplishments? _____

_____

Skills used? _____

_____

Major responsibilities? _____

_____

Promotions/awards/honors? _____

_____

Why did you leave this position? _____

Critical Incidents Worksheet

List critical incidents from each of your past jobs and what skills and/or achievements were involved.

Job	Incident	Skill/ Achievement

Note: Discretion is the better part of valor; I would hesitate to share with interviewers that such a legend is based on your actions because in the organization that you are meeting with, the employee may indeed get fired for such an "offense."

⭐ 8.1 Describe your current/last work group. What is/ What was it like working with your current/past work group?

This is an open-ended question to determine what characteristics the work group has that you feel important enough to disclose. Briefly mention the composition of the work group. Use major demographic categories—education level, gender, other EEO categories (marital status, race, national origin, age, religion)—whatever is appropriate to assist the interviewer to determine the kind of group you have experience working with. (Refer to page 159 for a related question asked in a more blatant way.) The more relevant the details, the more helpful your description is. Don't stop here. Go on to characterize the group in terms of the work situation—tight-knit, high work ethic, good-natured but serious about work—so that the interviewer is able to complete the picture and to compare it to the one you would be dealing with if a job were offered to you.

Avoid gossip or catty details. Applicants should avoid using the terms "girls," "guys," "gals," or "boys" entirely. "Colleagues," "associates," "the other men/ women" are terms that are much more professional and appropriate.

8.2 Let me describe the work group you would be joining if we asked you to fill the position. How would you fit in? In this position, how would you see your role as team member/builder?

The employer asks you to consider the circumstances and the environment of the workplace if the job is offered. You want to address this question whether or not the question is asked by the interviewer; you should be asking it of yourself. Can you see yourself working here, in this situation?

Use terms to describe your role in the work group: facilitator, leader, synthesizer, enabler, consensus builder, supporter. Use whatever term is an accurate, brief description of the role you played as a member of the team.

An aspect of this question not to be overlooked is that the answer requires you to possess a realistic understanding of the position and the work group. An example of a strong but brief answer is:

Since I have had experience in my last position starting a _____ department, being able to attend to details as well as to consider the human element gives me resources to draw upon in expanding the _____ area here.

8.3 What would be your ideal work group?

Be honest with yourself in your preparation for the interview. Be ready to answer this question, but remember that the reason for asking the question is to determine whether you are compatible with the work group that you would be joining if a job offer is extended. There are two approaches to this question.

1. If the employer has already shared with you his or her perceptions of the major characteristics of the work group, then you need to determine which of those elements are most compatible with yours. By identifying them, you are striving to demonstrate that there is a fit.

2. If the interviewer has not disclosed any characteristics of the work group, take a positive approach and, if it is perceived to be slightly ideal, that is fine. Here is an example.

My ideal work group would be one in which there is an infusion of a high work ethic throughout the group. Additionally, each of the participants has a real commitment to the work and to a high-quality product and a respect for each other and the organization they are a part of. The group is so effective in playing to strengths and supporting any weaknesses of the team members that the group actually performs with very little guidance and direction. If a problem arises, it is addressed and solved by the group itself.

☆ 8.4 How would you define a conducive work environment?

In addition to a description of the work group expand your answer to include:

… a supervisor who is a good communicator and enhances the productivity of the work group by sharing responsibility for output level and quality with each of the team members. He or she also realizes the importance of balancing task requirements with relationships. And last, an organization that values its employees.

8.5 Have you ever had to fire someone? Describe the circumstances and how you handled the situation.

Expect this question whenever you have disclosed on your resume and/or at your interview that you have managerial experience. Firing employees goes with the territory. If you have not fired anyone, the thinking is (and it is valid) that you have not had a complete management experience. (This alone doesn't make you a complete manager, but it is an experience without which it is difficult to demonstrate in-depth management experience.)

If you have never fired an employee, say so. If you were involved, regardless of the level, but not the decision maker, condition your response with the fact that you were part of the process and leave it at that.

The easiest answer is an affirmative one with no conditions or hedging. If you have done it, say so and stop. Terminating someone is one of the most difficult issues that a manager has to deal with for several reasons. If the termination is due to a staff restructuring or downsizing, you are required to sever someone's employment due to an elimination of the position and not due to the person's performance. (It seems though that great performers—except in the direst of circumstances—manage not to have their positions eliminated.) **Expressing sympathy with those whose jobs were lost and acknowledging the psychological and economic concerns shows that you do not take these tasks lightly.**

> *As _____ manager, I was often responsible for informing employees on my staff that, in line with the company's plan to curtail operations, a few of their positions were being eliminated. More often than not the handwriting was already on the wall, but in a few cases the employee was genuinely shocked. Fortunately, a generous severance package and outplacement counseling was being offered, but I found that very little could be done to soften the blow.*
>
> *Since I was in charge of the unit, I was responsible for the annual review of staff members. Several times I had to put employees on warnings for poor performance and then follow up with termination. In one case I was able to get the employee transferred to another area more suited to his skills.*
>
> *Our organization had a centralized human resource/personnel function and, although we recommended termination, they implemented the decision. Recommending termination was never an easy task.*

8.6 Have you ever had to hire someone? For what types of positions?
What do you look for when you hire someone?

> *Yes, regularly for _____ positions in our _____ department.*

If you feel you have not, **be careful before saying no** to this question. Were you involved in the hiring process, and are you now tempted to say no because you feel you were not the final determinant?

Remember also to recall circumstances when you were not an employee (for example, as a volunteer in a not-for profit organization or in a situation when you had to serve as a home care provider). In this situation, you may have had the opportunity to hire one or more individuals but you may not recall the situation because it occurred outside the workplace. Even though it occurred outside the workplace, the interviewer may relate to it.

This question demonstrates the seriousness of the person who is meeting with you. Expect the question to be raised in every situation where you will be expected to be involved in the hiring process. This is certainly true for applicants taking positions in the recruiting and selection (often called employment) area of human resource, as well as for others with hiring responsibility, usually manager level or above.

The characteristics frequently sought today are a strong work ethic, loyalty, knowledge, dedication, and experience. Another way to break it down is by starting with an overview statement:

> *Every potential employee we consider has "can do" and "will do" potential, and the purpose of the selection process is to make sure that the employee will be effective doing the job here.*

There may be a hidden agenda at work: defining your own hire. Are you strong on "will do" but do not have much experience to back you up? Stress that you look for potential; that you are hiring for today and for the future. If you have a varied background and are a chameleon in the workplace, say that you value "fit" because the interpersonal element is so important. This assumes that the basic job requirements ("can do")

Ingredients for a Successful Hire

"CAN DO"

Job candidate has the **ability** to do the job.
Has done the job in the past.

"WILL DO"

Job candidate's **effectiveness potential.**
Can do what we need here.

"FIT"

Job candidate comes from an
**organization/work group
similar to ours.**
Can be successful here.

have been met. With time and more recognition for the complexity of any job, it is difficult to conceive any recruiting and selection interview that does not attempt to identify the "will do" and "fit" categories in every candidate. To avoid questioning on these issues makes any hire more of a risk.

8.7 Have you ever had to motivate or build team spirit with co-workers? Describe why this happened.

Consider this an opportunity to obtain information about the organization and the work group you are going to be working with if an offer is extended. First you need to answer the question. You should be prepared for this question because of your review of your work experiences in detail before this meeting. Disclose the best situation that you were ever involved with, preferably as an employee but consider any team situation (including sports, by the way). Describe the circumstances briefly to show that you have leadership and take-charge ability (as well as the skill to analyze situations to determine when "soft" leadership skills and intuition are required). Once you have answered the question, add without pausing, *"Tell me if that same skill will be required here?"* Wait for the response without another word regardless of the length of time before the interviewer replies. The longer the silence, the more important the answer is.

☆ 8.8 Have you ever worked for a difficult person?

Do not get philosophical about all the various shades of meaning of the word "difficult," but realize that, once you start to answer, you have essentially assumed that the other person was "difficult" while you were not. You can avoid the dilemma by starting with, *"If by difficult you mean a person who _____, then, yes I have."* Examples may include a person who:

❏ Never allowed a typographical error.

❏ Set impossible deadlines all the time.

❏ Needed to make all the decisions.

❏ Trusted no one to take responsibility for anything.

❏ Would never delegate.

When answering, make sure the **difficulty is obvious and simple to describe,** as well as **likely to generate agreement from the interviewer.** Be on the lookout for gray areas that may cause confusion. One possibility is a "clean desk" (or "messy desk") person unless you are fairly certain that you and the interviewer are on the same page of the issue you introduce.

8.9   *How many of your bosses were male? Female? Were most of your co-workers male or female [or in other EEO categories]?*

This question should have been addressed in your review of your experience. Usually it is asked of the applicant who possesses an opposite characteristic (that is, a woman might be asked how many of her bosses/co-workers were men). Interviewers ask the question if they feel the need to determine whether you have had any experience in that kind of environment. If you have, be direct and positive: *"I have had three female bosses [co-workers], and each was a very positive experience as you will see when you check my references."*

   If you have not, say so but try to qualify it.

> *Although I have not had the opportunity to work for a female supervisor directly, in meetings and with clients I have dealt with women in supervisory capacities.*

> *All of the supervisors in my department are men, but I have had many professional dealings with women in other departments and in coordinating projects. I feel the key to any supervisor/subordinate relationship is a variety of factors but a primary one is the work ethic and therefore I am confident that will not be a problem.*

8.10   *How much time on your current/last job is/was spent working alone?*

The purpose of the question is to further the interviewer's understanding of the work environment and the nature of your job. Ideally look for balance between doing your own work alone and in the presence of others. By showing balance, you eliminate the opportunity for the interviewer to dismiss your application because the job available is the opposite of the situation you describe. Be ready for the next obvious question that in all probability follows: *"Which do you prefer?"* State simply that either is an effective environment for you unless you feel strongly that one works and the other doesn't. In that case state it directly and wait for the interviewer's response. If the situation is the opposite of your strong preference, it may be a deal-breaker. But if you are sure that it is, then do not backtrack, thereby allowing the interviewer to perceive you as weak.

8.11   *How often did you meet with your supervisor? For what purpose?*

This direct question is an opportunity for interviewers to determine what supervisory style you have been working under and gives them an opportunity to determine the extent of your autonomy.

We met at the start of each day to determine our priorities and identify what was to be accomplished that shift.

8.12 In your current/past position, how important is/was communication and dealing with others?
In your current/past position, what role does/did communication play?

Communication is being regarded as increasingly important in every organization. The interviewer is asking you to show your regard for it as well. Any answer with *"Not very important"* anywhere in it is perceived as weak and you with it. Regardless of the position, level of position, organization, industry, or sector, you need to be convinced of the importance communication plays in every position.

Communication was very important in my last position because to complete our work successfully, we needed to learn of any changes from the _____ department as quickly as they occurred, or else errors would result.

8.13 What form of communication do you prefer? Which do you feel is most effective?

Think about the ideal communication environment before you respond. *"What is the easiest form of communication?"* is the way the question would probably be phrased if you were looking at the same kind of question in a college communications course. Consider the choices: verbal and nonverbal communication. Of the two, obviously **verbal is less likely to cause misunderstanding.**

With regard to verbal communication, there are two types: oral (in the workplace the two major categories are face-to-face and telephone) and written. Rank them from easiest to most difficult. If you follow the same order as written in the preceding sentence, you agree with everyone that, unless there are mitigating circumstances (for example, two people who grow incensed anytime they meet), face-to-face communication is the most effective. It is the most direct and allows for the participants to be sensitive to the nonverbal messages and nuances.

Any reply that states written communication is the one you prefer or the most effective raises concern with most interviewers. The best interviewers probe to learn more about the answer. Others consider the answer as one from a person who prefers protocol and procedure to take precedence over effective communication.

I have always found that direct conversations have been the most effective, with occasional written follow-ups.

⭐ *8.14   Describe how your last/current job relates to the*
           overall goals of your department and organization.

All employees, regardless of level, should be aware of the roles their positions play in the goals of the department and how their department relates to the goals of the organization. This relates directly to "value-
added"—what value do you add to the organization? This should be true
for the not-for-profit, the public, and, of course, the private sectors.

> *Since I was the budget officer, every department relied on my monthly re-*
> *ports to analyze if they were meeting or exceeding projections. In turn, I was*
> *reliant on the various departments for submitting accurate production re-*
> *ports on a timely basis. It became a real team effort because there was a prof-*
> *it-sharing incentive in place, so everyone wanted to control expenses and in-*
> *crease production.*

⭐ *8.15   Do/Did you work on major projects in your current/*
           most recent job? Tell me about a project in your
           current/last job that you really got excited about?
           What were/are the most important projects completed
           on your last/current job?

Again, regardless of job level, use your Experience Worksheet (page 93) and
Critical Incidents Worksheet (page 94) prior to your interviews to determine
the aspects of your position that are project-oriented (vs. process-oriented or
operational). If you feel that none of your projects qualifies in the interviewer's perception as "major," then preface your remarks with that comment: *"I
don't think any of the projects that I have participated in will qualify as 'major.'
Nonetheless, let me tell you about this one that was essential to...."*

If you are at a loss and cannot think of any project at all in your current
job, think about your outside and family activities. Be careful not to over-
look relocations, long-term care considerations, selecting a college, planning a wedding (even a vacation!), a mortgage closing, or providing leadership for an event. (There are people all over the country who take
responsibility for chairing fundraising events that are as large and complex except those of the largest organizations. Don't forget to mention one
that you took responsibility for.)

Until very recently in the workplace, projects were not given the status
and consideration they warrant. Frequently, being placed on a special
project was a euphemism for being shown the door. The project skills
that one develops are an essential part of the baggage that professionals
bring with them to the workplace, and the skills required to bring a project to a successful completion are certainly traits to be recognized and
valued. With all the reorganizing throughout the United States, those
able to be effective in project assignments bring with them a package of

skills that are going to be a real asset in the organization's efforts to maximize its effectiveness.

8.16 How do you plan and organize for a major/ long-range project?

Here use your planning and organizing experience as a reference point to discuss the question in a most effective manner. It does not matter whether the project you are discussing was in or outside work, what is important is that you demonstrate that quickly and briefly you know how to plan and organize for a major long-range project. This is an opportunity for a tag question. At the end of your answer be sure to add (if you feel comfortable in doing so), *"Will there be opportunities for me to use these skills in the position we are discussing?"* This tag-on gets you more details on the scope and nature of the position.

8.17 How many projects can you handle at one time?

You need to balance and hedge. You do not want to portray yourself as a slave who takes an increasing burden of projects and never says no, but you want to demonstrate that you devour work and love the opportunity to be of assistance. A careful answer starts with a review of your own experience to determine what your experience has been.

> *I have had overlap in projects in the past that were completed according to schedule because I had the resources, both personnel and materials, needed to do so.*

> *Part of my credibility is my practice to never accept more than I anticipate I will with reasonable certainty be able to complete effectively and on schedule.*

8.18 What activities did/do you perform on your last/ current position and what was/is the approximate time devoted to these activities?

Consider this a request for a mini job description. When approximate time is requested, percentages work effectively.

If the job is directly tied to time of day and the work is fairly consistent on a daily basis, then choose a time format.

> *I usually reserved the first part of the morning for going through mail, reports, and returning telephone calls. Late mornings I would visit the manufacturing floor, touching base with the various section heads. Any problems would permit me to schedule a meeting after lunch to discuss in detail with the appropriate divisions. Afternoons were divided between telephone follow-ups with clients and suppliers, keeping appointments, and weekly meetings with senior management.*

For percentage:

> *Approximately 30 percent of my day was spent calling vendors to ensure that delivery dates continued to be firm. Another 30 percent was spent researching new product possibilities. About 15 percent was for correspondence, 5 percent was for our intern. The last 20 percent was reserved for meetings inside and outside the organization.*

Notice that no percentage is less than 5 percent and that the total comes to 100 percent.

8.19 What was/is your workload like on your last/ current job?

Now is not the time to complain about how unreasonable they were at your last place of employment. If the workload was heavy, say so and provide a few brief details to support your opinion. Relate the details, if possible, to the open position you are interviewing for:

> *As in your organization, when we approached the publication date, work escalated and overtime was often required. There was a definite ebb and flow to the workload, with some months, like our double holiday issue, especially frantic, coming at that time of year. The key to my being able to handle the extra work was expecting it to come because it always did.*

☆ 8.20 What were/are your most important decisions on your last/current job?

Take a matter-of-fact tone and identify the aspects of your job that gave you the opportunity to make meaningful decisions. The level of the position dictates the weight of the decision. It is perfectly acceptable (in fact, it may be encouraged) to identify the opportunity to make decisions slightly beyond the expected scope of the position, but it is folly to identify as important decisions clearly below your station. A vice-president may readily mention a "$2 million credit authority level" and an assembly line worker may mention the authority to shut the line down. However, the administrative assistant who takes credit for an increase in sales or a department manager who boasts about the annual picnic or the quarterly fire drill is not regarded favorably by the interviewer.

8.21 In what ways has your current/last job prepared you to take on greater responsibility?

By reviewing the experiences you encountered during your stay on your last job, you may now well reflect on what your next job should be. The more the situation is similar (if not identical) to the position you are interviewing for, the more the interviewer considers the "fit."

> *When my immediate supervisor was called away for jury duty, it was even longer than anticipated; he was sequestered for several weeks! During his absence I was responsible for running the division and I enjoyed it immensely. Deadlines and production adhered to schedule.*

8.22 Describe a situation when you had to make a "seat of the pants," quick decision.

Preferably this is an opportunity to describe a situation at work although, if you cannot think of one at work, take it from personal experiences. The goal of this question is to determine the ability of the applicant to make a reasonable decision quickly when there is no one to turn to. Be careful to not show yourself as someone who makes the decision to release a nuclear bomb but who is not afraid to make a decision if some risk is involved and who recognizes when more risk is involved in making no decision at all.

> *When serving as a lifeguard, even though there was no lightning, once the rain started I ordered the pool abandoned because two days before in another pool nearby a child had been struck by lightning under the same circumstances.*

⭐ 8.23 How were you evaluated on your last/current job?

Be brief and honest. Do not elaborate on an issue that you may be particularly sensitive to. **Clarify whether you are being asked about the method of evaluation or about your evaluation.**

> *We were on an MBO (management by objectives) system and had goals reviewed and updated every quarter.*
>
> *It is hard to say because I was there three years and never got a review.*
>
> *I was fortunate because I was aware of the fact that I should get periodic feedback. So I asked my supervisor during one of our one-on-one weekly meetings to tell me the strong and weak elements of my performance from the preceding week. She seemed to like my approach and I certainly appreciated her frank and timely comments.*

8.24 What are some things that you find difficult to do? Why?

Identify job elements that are perceived as tedious and of minor importance to the interviewer:

> *With everything else going on, I sometimes find it difficult to find the time to file.*

Keeping up with paperwork is sometimes difficult if not impossible because new orders are coming in all the time.

Or take a positive twist and make it a positive "problem."

Because service is such an important hallmark of our approach to internal as well as external customers, I find it difficult to say no even when the issue raised is not directly related to what we do but I know I can be of service.

I get so involved, it is tough to stop at the end of the day.

Because our customers are so valuable, I find it difficult to not be able to help them when an issue comes up that is outside our area.

8.25 *How do you remain effective when you are faced with difficult tasks or with things you do not like to do?*

Consider your worksheet to review which aspects of your most recent position you enjoy doing and which you do not. Consider your responsibilities also in terms of difficult versus "easy" tasks. People in the organizing and time management industry all encourage the completion of the most difficult and least liked tasks before the completion of any others (since if you put them off, chances are you will run out of time before you are able to deal with them).

8.26 *How would you rank yourself among your peers?*

One of the most difficult things for Americans to do is speak about themselves with a balance that positions us neither too low (most of us portray ourselves on a lower level than we should) or too high (which presents us in a boastful way). This is what makes the question a difficult one. At the same time you must remember that if you are not going to be your own cheerleader, who will? Can you offer concrete examples of your standing with awards such as "Employee of the Month" or "Division IV Sales Leader" or with instances where you were singled out to teach new employees or serve on a special committee? If so, share the information.

Cushion your answer, if you prefer, by saying *"I believe you will find when checking with my references that I am among the top quadrant in _____ when compared with my peers."* To put yourself in a lower category runs the risk of being considered an also-ran by the interviewer. For the most careful and honest answer, consider the aspects of your ability that you are best at, and then look at those where you could stand improvement. Practice saying both before the meeting. Listen and get others' opinions to determine how "honest" you need to be without appearing untruthful to yourself.

☆ **8.27 *Draw an organization chart showing the positions that you reported to and interacted with on a regular basis in your last/current position. Describe the organizational structure in which you are now working/worked last.***

If you do not have an organization chart to review from your last/current position, make one now before the interview. This is an excellent way to review all the intricacies of your last or current position. You can use a format similar to that in the Organization Chart (below). Leave off names

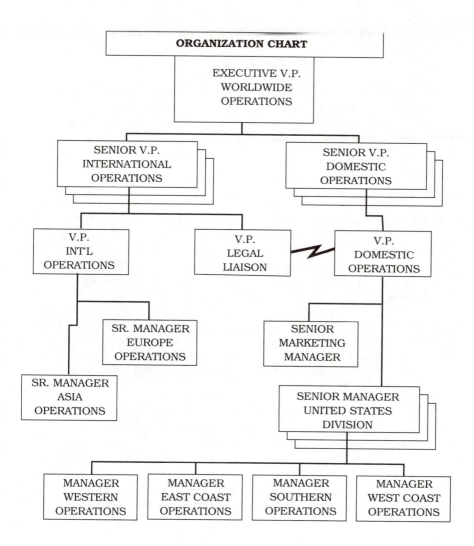

ORGANIZATION CHART

EXECUTIVE V.P.
WORLDWIDE
OPERATIONS

SENIOR V.P.
INTERNATIONAL
OPERATIONS

SENIOR V.P.
DOMESTIC
OPERATIONS

V.P.
INT'L
OPERATIONS

V.P.
LEGAL
LIAISON

V.P.
DOMESTIC
OPERATIONS

SR. MANAGER
EUROPE
OPERATIONS

SENIOR
MARKETING
MANAGER

SR. MANAGER
ASIA
OPERATIONS

SENIOR MANAGER
UNITED STATES
DIVISION

MANAGER
WESTERN
OPERATIONS

MANAGER
EAST COAST
OPERATIONS

MANAGER
SOUTHERN
OPERATIONS

MANAGER
WEST COAST
OPERATIONS

and include corporate and functional titles (or just functional titles if you prefer, never just corporate titles). "Vice-president" doesn't say anything about the type or level of responsibility; "Vice-President Marketing, North American Region" does.

This, as well as other exercises listing prior jobs, responsibilities, and/or data regarding your professional history, should provide insights for you as well as jog your memory. It may be that you never considered certain reporting relationships being keys to performing your job or that "looking at the big picture" may stimulate your thoughts as to the type of organization and position you prefer.

How does your current or prior organization compare with the organization that you are interviewing with? If you do not know, it is logical for you to ask as long as the interviewer brought up the subject. Point out any positive parallels.

> *With the last two foreign banks that I worked at I became very flexible about frequent changes in senior management. I found one key to my success was to remain nonpolitical and show loyalty to the company. As you are part of an international corporation, I imagine the turnover may be quite similar.*

8.28 *Have you ever changed the nature of your job? How?*

With all the reorganizing taking place in the workplace, in addition to the popularity of self-directed work teams, it is quite possible that you had the opportunity to participate in the reorganization of your own job. If you have, say so and describe the details briefly. Any positive answer, either in professional or personal life, shows your creativity and problem-solving ability.

8.29 *Have you ever had to make an unpopular decision/ announcement? Describe it and tell me how you handled it.*

A review of your Experience Worksheet or Critical Incidents Worksheet may identify when you had to make an unpopular decision. Now is the time to share it with your interviewer. Do not consider only major situations. Even if as a clerk you needed to bring a matter to the attention of your supervisor risking the wrath of your co-workers, now is the time to mention it. **Employers look for loyalty to the organization and supervisors, combined with real experience with tough situations.**

⭐ **8.30 In your current/past position, how many levels of management do/did you have to communicate with? On what issues and levels do/did you deal with management?**

The interviewer is trying to determine the range of your contacts in your last position. In an effort to give substance to your answer, and also as a reality check, provide the functional and corporate title (never the name) and briefly describe the purpose and extent of the contact.

In addition to the ongoing contact with the Vice-President for Manufacturing, and the District Sales Manager, I had to deal with the relocation officer for a major move our department was going through and see the CFO monthly for budget variances.

8.31 In your current/past position, what problems did you identify that had previously been overlooked?

Here is a chance to shine by being prepared. *The interviewer is trying to determine your ability to see beyond the confines of the day-to-day activities of the position to significantly improve the position's output and effectiveness.* **A major reason for bringing someone in to fill a position from the outside is to get a fresh look at the situation and bring new ideas.** You want the interviewer to think "can do" and "will do," and raise the hope that you have new solutions in your repertoire.

8.32 On what basis were/are you able to determine if you were doing a good job on your last/current job?

This should be a cakewalk of a question, but unfortunately it frequently is not. All employees, regardless of job position, location, industry, or sector, should be able to assess their own performance level periodically. If workers do not do this, they are at the mercy of the person who evaluates them. A proactive stance in performance appraisal is recommended. **By periodically determining the level of your own performance, you become a consistent benchmark and evaluator of your own performance.**

8.33 What determines progress in a good organization?

Increasingly important assignments, recognition of one form or another, a personal feeling of accomplishment are all characteristics that would imply progress in a good organization.

8.34 What do you think is the most difficult aspect of being a manager/executive?

"Giving bad news" is as succinct and to the point as one can get. This answer provides a brief valid answer that begs the serious interviewer to ask you for more. A superficial interviewer does not pursue with additional questions to flesh out your thought-provoking response and to determine whether there is substance and a demonstration of in-depth experience behind the answer. This response addresses how a manager reacts to difficult situations.

A second response demonstrates that the manager is ready to take control and provide leadership from the start. *"Getting the group of people that you have inherited to respond quickly and effectively to your authority."*

Motivating people and finding (as well as building) the team are additional areas to explore in finding an effective approach to this question. Both certainly demonstrate to the interviewer the depth of your experience and your ability to be trusted with the responsibility for managing others.

8.35 What do you think makes this position different from your last/current position?

Look for a positive trait that distinguishes the two. If that positive trait demonstrates that you will be a strong employee, then you are successfully answering the question.

The work group is more committed.
The management appears more supportive.
The challenges are greater.

8.36 What do you wish you had accomplished at your last/current position that you were unable to?

"A promotion, a new assignment, a relocation" all have to do with your positioning. Another approach is to target specific changes in the process: *"The introduction of new technology, a turnaround time of less than 20 minutes, lower turnover."* These are all perfectly acceptable alternatives because they allow the interviewer to think again "can do–will do."

8.37 What kind of decisions are most difficult for you?

Identify those that involve either a human relations issue or a lower or subordinate level. Concentrate on those dealing with tough choices:

Do I give the person another chance who has just broken the machinery for the third time?

Do I vote to close the plant because for the last three quarters productivity has been falling and one of four plants must be closed?

☆ 8.38 What makes you think you could handle a position that requires so many diverse talents and persuasive skills?

This question is a positive alternative to the query *"You don't seem to have all the experience I want, why should I hire you?"* Even when presented with the question in this way, reply alertly. Break the question into two parts so that you are not tempted to make a long boring statement. You also have the added benefit of drawing the interviewer into concurrence with your reply.

Start by saying, *"In my opinion, this position requires the following talents and skills.... Correct?"* List them briefly and stop. If you do this in a gentle way, you get the interviewer's buy-in.

Proceed carefully in case interviewers are distracted or feel that you are now quizzing them. The second reason to be extremely careful is so that, when listing the talents and skills (in addition to persuasive skills), you select and emphasize those that play to your strengths. Avoid making a list emphasizing that the job may overwhelm you.

> *I feel that my current position has many demands for skills, and I have been able to meet the demands thus far with great success. My special ability to be a quick learner and intuitive about other people's ability has enabled me to react to situations as needed.*

If the interviewer cites a skill that you apparently do not have and that is felt to be essential to the position, unless it is an obvious one, ask what aspect of the job requires it. You may cause the interviewer to rethink the job, reconsider the job requirements, or open the door to alternative skills or experience that you do have.

> *It is true that I do not have hands-on experience with WordPerfect but Word for Windows is so similar I feel confident that it will not take any time to be proficient. In fact, current upgrades make the two programs even more compatible.*

8.39 What would you do if you had to make a decision without a procedure or precedent to guide you?

This is a question to determine whether you have the ability to think for yourself and on your own two feet. The question is posed to determine your level of flexibility. **Do you need rules all the time or will you be lost?**

Are you the kind of person who will blend into our environment? You will have prepared for this question, when reviewing your experience, by considering what environment you prefer to work in: one with few rules and the excitement of the unknown or a more staid environment where rules and procedures provide a very structured environment for conducting business.

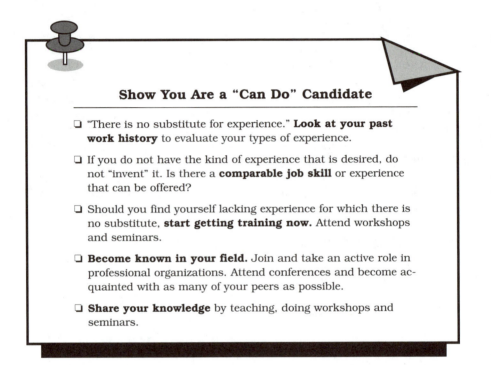

Show You Are a "Can Do" Candidate

❑ "There is no substitute for experience." **Look at your past work history** to evaluate your types of experience.

❑ If you do not have the kind of experience that is desired, do not "invent" it. Is there a **comparable job skill** or experience that can be offered?

❑ Should you find yourself lacking experience for which there is no substitute, **start getting training now.** Attend workshops and seminars.

❑ **Become known in your field.** Join and take an active role in professional organizations. Attend conferences and become acquainted with as many of your peers as possible.

❑ **Share your knowledge** by teaching, doing workshops and seminars.

9

Behavior Questions

How Are Your People Skills?

One increasingly popular way of determining a candidate's effectiveness is with the use of behavioral questions. Those proponents of the behavioral approach contend that **past performance is the best predictor of future performance** ("can do"–"will do" again). In behavioral questioning, the interviewer asks applicants to supply experiences with situations that they will face if offered a position with the organization.

Behaviors are actions (or reactions) in a situation. There are three aspects to a job:

❑ Skill assessment

❑ Motivation

❑ "Fit" or emotional quotient

When trying to determine the prospective effectiveness of an applicant, employers must consider all three elements of the job. Skill assessment may be discussed in the interview process but that skill (which could be mentioned on a resume or job application) should be tested more specifically because talk is a poor substitute for action. Applicants can say that they can operate a piece of equipment, but the employer never knows until they are hired if they can really do it—unless a work sample test is provided during the selection process. Motivation and fit are the two other elements that should be assessed during the interview process.

One way to prepare for questions in this area is to consider all the "behaviors" that you (and you hope the organization) feel to be essential to the job. *Behaviors are activities that are required for effective job performance.* Examples of activities such as filing, sorting, and listing need to be given more detail to constitute specific examples from your past when you exhibited these behaviors. What was filed, how they were received, and why they were stored would all be included. Additionally, the technology would be discussed, and details would be provided to describe whether they were filed on microfiche, microfilm, or with a scanner and PC software.

What distinguishes questions about behaviors from the "personal" questions discussed in Chap. 6? **Behavioral questions are work-based and try to link past job applicant behavior to behaviors required in the organization conducting the interview.** They constitute a unique form of questioning that determines whether past behaviors in similar or identical situations are clues to future performance in the environment for which the candidate is being considered. The hypothesis obviously is that there are real links.

If you have details about the position or if you can hypothesize about the behaviors needed in the position, you can prepare a Behavior Worksheet (page 115). List any and all essential behaviors in as much detail as you can about the position for which you are applying. Next, consider the relative importance of each of these behaviors to the organization and rank them. In the column next to each behavior, cite a job or situation from your experience that also required that behavior and that you were able to perform. This chart can point up your "weak" spots and allows you to consider in advance how your strengths and weaknesses may affect your "fit" to the position. Do not concentrate only on task-related behaviors such as answering telephones, using a fax machine, or being able to type 60 wpm; include other important behaviors such as delegating, scheduling, and organizing. When considering the behaviors required in the open position, look for alternatives in your own background. For example, you may have not worked as a receptionist per se but have done telemarketing that requires telephone and communication skills.

☆ 9.1 What is your management style? Provide examples from your current (or most recent) position that demonstrate this style.

You should have already considered this question as part of a self-assessment in preparation for any job search effort. *There are two major approaches: One emphasizes task and the other stresses relationships.* They are not necessarily mutually exclusive, nor should they ever be, according to the management experts. In the traditional sense, managers were portrayed in a maintenance mode and reactive in a bureaucratic setting; leaders, on the other hand, were proactive, looked for problems and issues before they occurred, and were results-driven and entrepreneurial in thinking.

Behavior Worksheet

Organization: _____

Position: _____

Rank behaviors from most essential (#1) to least essential (#5)

Essential Behaviors Required in Position	Ranking	Examples Date & Job

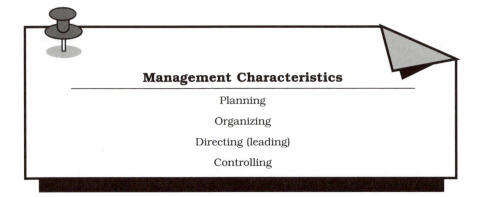

Management Characteristics

Planning

Organizing

Directing (leading)

Controlling

The four major characteristics (planning, organizing, directing, and controlling) seem to have survived the test of time; various management theories may be considered within this context and still be complete. TQM (total quality management), reengineering, and benchmarking are all tools for managers to use when executing one of their major functions and can be found in the titles of many recent best sellers on management.

"Leadership," on the other hand, has become a popular term to suggest the new approach that effective managers must now embrace if they are to be effective in this new highly competitive environment with a diverse workforce taking a global approach to the marketplace. Interviewers may use the terms "manager" and "leader" interchangeably. So clarify which you are talking about if you feel you and the interviewer are not both discussing the same attributes.

With that as background, think about your management style before the interview. Use the Are You a Manager or a Leader? questionnaire (page 117) to help you consider the differences in approach. The higher the position you are interviewing for, the more insightful you are expected to be. Even if this is an entry-level position, be ready with an answer.

To prepare for this question, first consider the traits of the persons you most remember as great managers and what made them great. Think also about terrible managers for whom you worked and what made them terrible. Then move on to yourself. Regardless of your level professionally, consider a situation where you had the opportunity to get things done through others (that's what management is all about) and recall what made you effective or ineffective. Did you communicate effectively? Stress teamwork? Emphasize quality and/or results? Did you get your hands dirty? Now try an answer that says yes to all these:

I am a hands-on manager who stresses the importance of ongoing communication in building a team that delivers quality results.

Are You a Manager or a Leader?

Compare column A to column B. For each row mark a Yes for the statement that your work style agrees with.

A	or	B
____ Do you work within boundaries?		____ Do you expand boundaries?
____ Do you control resources?		____ Do you influence others?
____ Are you making plans to reach goals?		____ Are you working to create a future?
____ Are you responsible for when and how work is done?		____ Do you commit to get the work done at any cost?
____ Are you ruled by reason and logic supported by intuition?		____ Are you ruled by intuition and feelings supported by reason?
____ Do the past and precedents dictate present actions?		____ Does your vision for the future dictate present actions?
____ Do you make decisions only after all relevant information is available?		____ Do you decide when you feel you have enough (not all) information?
____ Do you measure performance against plans?		____ Do you measure accomplishments against vision of the future?

Scoring: Yes answers in column A indicate Management qualities, while those in column B pertain to Leadership.

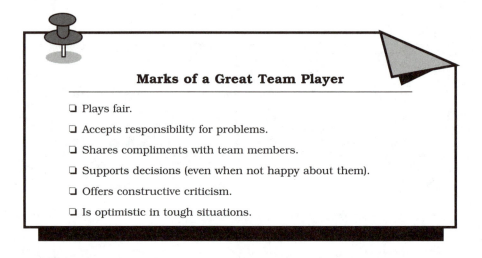

Marks of a Great Team Player

❏ Plays fair.

❏ Accepts responsibility for problems.

❏ Shares compliments with team members.

❏ Supports decisions (even when not happy about them).

❏ Offers constructive criticism.

❏ Is optimistic in tough situations.

One last comment on using the term "leadership." Leadership is really the third characteristic of the management function, the one responsible for directing (or leading) the activities of others. It becomes the characteristic of particular importance when talking about a participatory style of management because, rather than just expecting the workers to "do," it involves employees in the organizing, planning, and control aspects of the function. What, then, is left for the manager to do? Direct or lead.

Use the word "we" rather than "I" to demonstrate that you give credit for accomplishments to the team that you say is so important to your managerial effectiveness (if that is what you mentioned). A survey recently reported in the media states that 57 percent of executives feel that having poor team playing skills is the easiest way to kill a career.

9.2 Are you a good manager? Give some examples showing that you are a good manager.

Consider each of the four major functions cited earlier and determine which best brings out examples to demonstrate your management ability.

Relocation expenses were out of control when I took responsibility for the function. I reviewed the reports [control]*, and worked with seasoned staff to determine the key entry points to maximize efforts and contain expenses. They made a series of recommendations* [direct] *and we drafted a plan. We then set up a work flow system to maximize the effectiveness of the new procedures* [organize]*.*

Say no and you won't get the job—unless, just occasionally, the astute interviewer is asking the question because the last thing the organization wants is a good manager. Most organizations want hands-on persons who do the job themselves. Even in this situation, it is safer to say:

> *I am good at both—being a good manager and being a "solo practitioner."*
> *I have been in both situations throughout my career and have learned to be effective at both.*

Do not panic if you never managed in a paid capacity; chances are that you have done so either personally with your family or as part of voluntary or community activities. Prepare before the meeting to identify situations that you were personally involved in that demanded management expertise. If you are a recent college graduate, consider any organizations you held a title in or any activities (a dance, raffle, concert) that you actively worked to promote. Determine which of those duties you performed required help from others.

9.3 *Are you a persistent person? Describe an incident from your current/past job that supports this opinion.*

This is a fine-line question because what is perceived to be persistent to one person may be regarded as stubborn, inflexible, or argumentative by someone else. What is persistence? Let us define it here as *the ability and desire of a person to stick with an issue until its resolution (which may include acceptance or rejection).* If rejection is the decision, additional persistence may or may not be a positive characteristic, and the judgment of the person involved becomes increasingly a major issue.

Is persistence a positive characteristic? Regardless of the intent of the interviewer, start with your positive spin on the characteristic and pay particularly close attention to the interviewer to determine his or her opinion and feelings about persistence. You may start by saying:

> *First let me share my bias. I feel that to be effective in an organization a certain amount of persistence is required.*

Then proceed to say:

> *In answer to your question I am a persistent person. Let me give you a situation that demonstrates my use of persistence to complete a project.*

Then you move on to the second part of the question and tell about what action you performed that demonstrates your persistence in a favorable light. For example, a woman told this story recently:

> *After making a deposit at my bank (one of the biggest in the country) through a cash machine, I noticed that my account was never credited. A visit to the*

bank provided no satisfaction and it was obvious, after three attempts in two different areas of the bank that the staff at the branch had suggested, that nothing was going to be done. After considering whether anyone else at the bank could help me, I realized I only knew a vice-chairman who I went to high school with. But that was twenty years ago and we were never anything more than casual acquaintances. Desperate to get my money, I wrote him a letter. A few weeks later, one night our dinner was interrupted by a telephone call from him. He apologized for the delay in his response but wanted to tell me to call his assistant the next day to resolve the problem. It was solved immediately and my account credited. It is a good thing I did what I did because a few days later I received one of those computerized responses from the area I had been initially asked by the branch to work with. They informed me that a thorough investigation had led them to the conclusion that my claim was without merit. I sent their written conclusion to the vice-chairman along with my thank you note. I am so glad I had gone to him in spite of the branch's reassurances.

That story brings out a few issues that make the interviewer consider her favorably. First, this was a story *most individuals could relate to.* Second, *persistence permeates the story.* The woman had persistence in getting the deposit credited to her account as she should have and the persistence is moderate but effective. Third, the storyteller demonstrates quite visibly her *project orientation, results-based approach, problem-solving and creative skills*—all of which are job-related. Fourth, she shows with the thank you letter her professional courtesy and her interest in providing *effective follow-up* and feedback. In short, she says a lot with her brief vignette. The key is to provide an example that the interviewer can relate to and to resolve a problem that begs for a solution but that a less persistent person would not pursue.

☆ 9.4 How do/did you interact differently with diverse management levels and types?

You need to show that you are accustomed to interacting with different management levels. Refresh your memory by reviewing your Experience Worksheet (page 93) and the Organization Chart (page 107).

Indicate with a brief answer the variety of unit heads that you have had to deal with and for what issues.

9.5 How far do you see yourself rising in our organization?

Be realistic. If you can be vague and you want to take that tack, certainly do so. *"I would like to rise as high as my skills and opportunities here permit."* If it works and there is no follow-up question, you are off the hook and chances are the interviewer is either distracted or very inexperienced and/or untrained. Chances are that you need to provide a little more detail.

Consider your field of expertise as one avenue: *"I would like to eventually be responsible for the marketing function, or become CFO, or any other title head for a major function, or even chairman of the board."* Make sure that the goal is appropriate and that you feel confident sharing this information with the interviewer.

☆ 9.6 *What is your relationship with your former employer?*

"We continue to keep in touch," is a nice way to start if that is the truth. If it isn't, do not worry because a continuing relationship with a former employer is, under usual circumstances, as difficult to maintain as a relationship with a divorced spouse. *"We haven't spoken* [or better *we have occasionally spoken*] *since I left, but they know they are free to call if a situation requires my attention."* Sometimes an employer of a departing employee invites the exemployee back for consulting assignments. If this is true, say so because this scenario suggests a real respect for the applicant and that message will be heard.

Note: Keep this in mind if you have not left your job yet. As part of the agreement, especially if it is employer-initiated, ask if you would be considered for consulting assignments and discuss the process of consultant selection in detail.

☆ 9.7 *Describe a situation when the team fell apart. What was your role in the outcome?*

Do not be concerned here about the "failure" aspect of the question. The interviewer wants an idea, based on your experience, how you deal with adversity: *first, that you recognize problems when they occur and, second, that you are able do something about them.*

For example, a manager of a training facility for a major New York City bank was unable to solve serious attendance problems with his group of more than 20 instructors who were primarily single parents. The problem was not just one of replacement requirements when an instructor was late or took an unscheduled day off, but the amount of bickering among the workers increased as the problem intensified. Desperate to do something (you may not want to share that type of comment with the interviewer), he identified a two-pronged solution. First, he made one person responsible for time and attendance records; second, with his limited autonomy, he gave them an incentive that many would regard as puny. His incentive was simple: Any staff member with no lateness and no unexcused absence for a period of six months would be entitled to a half day off. He was the first to acknowledge this was not much of an award, but it worked because the staff really valued any time they had to themselves.

☆ **9.8   Describe a situation where the person you were dealing with enabled you to be more effective.**

Think win-win. Consider this example:

> *I joined a smaller, privately held entertainment company, after spending several years at a major, publicly traded music company with foreign ownership. Now, when I dealt with my direct report, the company's president, she was pleased at the swiftness of issue resolutions for major decisions involving the department's budget and marketing campaigns. Going from a pressure cooker environment to one where skills were appreciated and relationships could be developed was such a pleasure. This was due to the quick, positive response by the president to my efforts.*

☆ **9.9   Describe a situation where you needed to get an understanding of another's viewpoint before you could get your job done. What problems did you encounter and how did you handle them?**

Consider a situation when you and a colleague had a major difference of opinion regarding an action plan or a definition of a problem that you were both expected to solve. This kind of scenario frequently serves to address this question. What frequently exacerbates the problem is a personality conflict, and the working relationship may be marred by nonwork-related issues. Whatever you do, *never identify a scenario that may lead the interviewer to think that you may be the problem,* because the questions raised about where the real problem lies are greater and more memorable than the issues the story is intended to resolve.

9.10   How did you feel the last time you joined a new organization and met your new group?

A balanced comment is a demonstration of a realistic approach on your part. You need to feel optimistic, but at the same time it is not surprising for you to detect a "show us" attitude.

9.11   How do/did you get along with your current/last work group?

Avoid negatives. If you have anything negative to say, it can only be done in the context of, *"I was much more interested in getting the job done than they were."* Otherwise, you were very effective in your dealings with them, and in fact there was real cohesion in the group. (Provide one or two examples of how the group clung together in a "crisis" situation.)

⭐ **9.12   Tell me about a difficult situation when you pulled the team together.**

Identify a situation that leads to a positive outcome and be careful during the answering of the question to mix your "we" and "I" pronouns to demonstrate that you were an active participant of the group.

> *When one of the members, and the most highly regarded, of our five-person team resigned, I had to break the news not only that was she leaving but that she would not be replaced. I then told the team that we would meet in two days to map out a strategy to determine how we were going to accomplish the same results with only four people. Then for the next two days (right up to the meeting), I visited each person (including the departing employee) to assess their morale and their level of concern—as well as their willingness to identify and participate in a new work process. Individually I mentioned to each of them that the business was going through a downturn and really needed each person's input and participation if we were to continue as a work group and help the organization to get through this difficult time in its life cycle. I must have gotten through because two of the members brought doughnuts and one of them stated at the beginning of the meeting how they had been discussing this situation among themselves and wanted me to know that they realized the tough situation I was in and that they were giving me their total support and attention because we were going to get through this together.*

9.13   When you begin to work with new people, how do you get to understand them? Are you successful in predicting/interpreting their behavior? Give examples.

Listening is the key to getting to understand another person. When you start with a new work group, they have an advantage over you: They need to understand just one person—you. You, on the other hand, must get to understand each and every one of them. Additionally, even with excellent listening skills, it is still difficult to predict a person's behavior each and every time. To answer this question in a strong, confident manner, it is important to say at the start that you have had a great deal of success predicting and interpreting other people's behavior but also mention that it does not always work. Then proceed with a brief example or two.

> *An MBA we had hired needed to be told that one of her responsibilities would include increased time on the switchboard. She said that she felt we were going to have this discussion and she realized that because we were short staffed she would be expected to put more time on phone coverage. This was not a surprise because during the recruiting and selection process we had emphasized in our discussions the "hands-on" and "do whatever we have to" atmosphere that is a key to the culture of our organization and she had confirmed throughout that she realized that this is something she may be called on to do once she joined us.*

☆ 9.14 Tell me about a responsibility in your current/last job that you really enjoyed.

Be careful not to throw this gift question away. Even though it should be easy, carefully determine your answer in advance. This is sometimes a "one-two" question that is immediately followed by a request for you to identify the responsibility you really liked least.

In an ideal situation, concentrate on the most important aspects of your position—the most creative, the most project-oriented, the most essential to the organization—or the aspects that provided you with the most visibility. A very senior member of the management of one of the world's major banks used to always say, *"An organization can never have enough good people. If you meet one as a job applicant and you don't have a job to offer, hire him or her, make the hire anyway, and find something for the person to do."* Too frequently, however, interviewers are more interested in screening out rather than screening in and *this question could be the decision maker.* If you are being considered for a position well below your last one, you may be giving the interviewer an opportunity to dismiss you.

☆ 9.15 Give an example where you had to be _____ on the job.

This question gives interviewers the opportunity to determine how you exhibit a certain characteristic that they feel is essential to the position. You should be well prepared for this question having reviewed the Behavior Worksheet. Given the list you prepared, what additional characteristics do you feel are essential to the job or detrimental to your candidacy?

Depending on the trait and the interviewer's agenda, *this question can either screen in or screen out candidates.* Traits can be viewed either as a positive or as a negative. Take, for example, the adjectives "creative" and "aggressive." Creativity in an advertising manager is a laudable trait; in an accountant, creative bookkeeping entries could cause problems. Aggressiveness in sales managers who push into new markets could be exactly what a start-up company needs, but aggressiveness is not what a child care agency requires. All positions should be viewed as offering opportunities to exhibit most personal traits, and can be a greater or lesser part of the position's responsibility. For the "creative" accountant, a response could be:

> *I find that all the different types of clients and their individual business needs require a creative mind to solve their problems. No two clients are alike, and I feel that my secret to my success is making them feel that they get individual service created for their individual needs.*

9.16 Describe a complex problem that you had to deal with.

To prepare an answer to this question, refer to your Experience Worksheet (page 93) and Critical Incidents Worksheet (page 94). When reviewing accomplishments, select one of the most meaningful and consider it from a level of complexity. Pick a situation that shows you to be an effective organizational player. For the word "problem" substitute "project" if it helps to clarify appropriate situations.

One HR professional recalls the story told by a Vietnam veteran who decided to defend a buddy of his who had been falsely accused of being AWOL while on a guard duty assignment. The vet told how with no legal training he identified the authorities he needed to deal with, conducted research, and, because of his warm manner, was able to get the charges swiftly dismissed. This is a good example that **not only brings out the complexity of the problem succinctly but incorporates the value of working relationships as well.**

9.17 Describe a situation where you failed to reach a goal.

Interviewers try to determine how you deal with adversity and see if you have a need to win every time. Identify a situation where you had to adjust your sights and, if possible, go back to succeed at a later date. Succeeding, however, is not as important as your demonstration of an ability to deal with tough times as well as good.

College may be one example, for instance, if you had to delay higher education because of personal circumstances. Do not let bitterness come through.

> *I had hoped to work at night while attending classes during the day to complete my college education, but the high cost of living caused me to have to work full-time just to support myself. I was fortunate to have an employer that switched my schedule to daytime and I attended classes in the evenings and weekends. It took me longer to get my degree but I always felt that I valued my education more because I really had to "earn" to learn. My business courses also related to my day-to-day activities on the job.*

> *I had submitted a training program proposal to a local bank at their request. Many meetings were held, with senior management requesting revisions in the program, which I accommodated. The meetings never resulted in a signed contract, however, because the HR manager quit the position in the midst of negotiations to work at another bank. The timing was not good to push the proposal forward at that time. A few years passed and the replacement's replacement, in cleaning out drawers, found my proposal. She contacted me, we had one meeting and then signed a contract. One point she made in discussing the original proposal with me was how willing I was to meet the specific needs of the bank.*

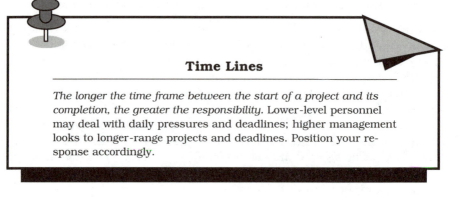

Time Lines

The longer the time frame between the start of a project and its completion, the greater the responsibility. Lower-level personnel may deal with daily pressures and deadlines; higher management looks to longer-range projects and deadlines. Position your response accordingly.

9.18   Describe circumstances where you had to work under pressure and deal with deadlines.

This should be an easy one for everyone, but do not take it for granted. Review your worksheets and consider the best, most recent story that the interviewer is most likely to relate to. If this is the essence of your daily activities, mention that fact and discuss the various deadlines and pressures you need to deal with on a regular and daily basis. This is as true, if not even more so, for those returning to the workplace. With many projects to deal with and soft lines of responsibility, the pressure may be greater and the deadlines sometimes ignored until a crisis develops.

If you cannot think of such a situation either at work or in your personal life, seek assistance from a relative, friend, or colleague. The experiences are there; it just takes sensitivity to identify them.

9.19   We have a continuing problem with _____. How would you handle this problem?

In this behavioral question, interviewers are asking you to demonstrate your specific work experience and mirror the situation they are describing. You need to focus on their description of the situation. Your answer not only has to demonstrate your comprehension of the question but briefly and succinctly provide a cogent answer as well. If the question includes *"requests to provide event tickets—especially at the last minute,"* give some suggestions that you would consider. If you have a "been there, done that" experience, now is the time to highlight it.

☆ 9.20   Describe what happened yesterday at work. Describe a typical day in your current/last position.

This great question offers you the opportunity to **define and establish the way you perceive your job in the most specific of terms**—one specific day's activities and accomplishments. Even though the question may ask for what happened yesterday, by preparing in advance you may want to consider using poetic license in your answer. The proviso is that the picture you present should be accurate even though the events and activities described did not happen yesterday. If you are concerned that you are not being entirely honest, mention that, *"Yesterday was a bit boring but let me describe one of the two more interesting issues that arise in my position quite frequently. They really didn't happen yesterday, but they will give you a better picture of the nature and scope of the position."* Give consideration to your experience worksheet to ensure that you include all the major activities, even if they are not done on a daily basis.

Practice the answer before any meeting to determine its length and range, keeping within the two-minute range. It is a good practice question because it keeps you aware of recent activities and current issues.

9.21 Describe a situation where you had a personal commitment that conflicted with an emergency business meeting. What did you do?

This question seeks to determine your level of loyalty. You need to answer directly and unhesitatingly.

I would have to make arrangements to be sure that the personal commitment is taken care of by someone else.

You may even add that:

I always try to warn anyone that I deal with outside the organization that any commitment is subject to change if my employer requires it.

If you have an example of a situation that shows what length your commitment to the organization is, give it. Here is one example:

I was a frequent workshop speaker for a major professional organization. They realized that I should have a back-up and they had found a few just to take care of such an emergency. While at a workshop I was required to return. Even though the professional organization had back-ups, none was available. To resolve the matter, I arranged a teleconference session in order to ensure that the professional organization met its commitment, but also and more importantly so that I was present for a meeting back at headquarters.

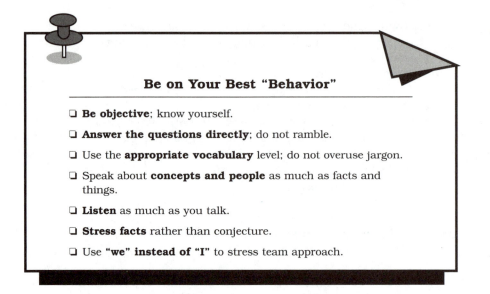

Be on Your Best "Behavior"

❏ **Be objective**; know yourself.

❏ **Answer the questions directly**; do not ramble.

❏ Use the **appropriate vocabulary** level; do not overuse jargon.

❏ Speak about **concepts and people** as much as facts and things.

❏ **Listen** as much as you talk.

❏ **Stress facts** rather than conjecture.

❏ Use **"we" instead of "I"** to stress team approach.

10
Stress Questions

Can You Take the Heat?

The Central Intelligence Agency and law enforcement agencies sometimes submit candidates to one or more stress tests to determine if the candidate is "tough enough" to handle a grueling job. As part of that assessment, candidates for positions in those organizations are sometimes subjected to stress interviews. Other organizations and individuals (not associated with the spying or law enforcement industries) also come to the conclusion that stress interviews are an effective technique to evaluate job candidates even though research results repeatedly demonstrate that stress interviews are not valid predictors of job performance.

Stress—the Ever Present Factor in the Employment Process

Whether the employer consciously decides to inject it or not, stress permeates the employment process in every organization as it attempts to find the right candidate for each position it seeks to fill.

The interview itself can be a stressful experience for any job candidate (not to mention, possibly, the interviewer). Additionally, the surroundings may contribute. Asking a job candidate to fill out an application without a clipboard or, worse, a pen may be an agonizing experience for the person who has no flat surface available to complete the application.

The furniture may also contribute to stress. A U.S. subsidiary of a major Japanese bank had futons available for job applicants in its

Human Resource reception area. There were no choices. It was futons or stand. They were easy enough to sit on and comfortable too. The problem with the futons, though, was that they were impossible to get up from without some very awkward moments for both male and female candidates.

The receptionist and other staff coming into contact with job candidates may provide additional opportunities for stress. There is the story of the HR vice-president who, when passing through the reception area for the third time in three hours, noticed the same person sitting in the same place. When she asked the receptionist why the applicant was still sitting there, he responded, "How should I know. If he doesn't know enough to come to me and give me his completed application, that's his problem." Even though the receptionist was let go the next day, it was one day too late for the erstwhile applicant. Other examples are the "front office" employees who are less than hospitable to the visitor. Before the interview even starts, candidates have to expend valuable energy and confidence to get to where they were supposed to be in the first place.

A lot of questions throughout this book (possibly all of them) may increase the stress level of the candidate. In this chapter we consider the questions that are the most stressful and intimidating, some intentionally so, as shown in the chart below.

Stress Makers	Stress Breakers
❏ The interview itself	❏ Prepare; know your material.
❏ Silence during the interview; internal pressure to keep on talking	❏ Accept silence; avoid being intimidated to speak more. Control disclosure.
❏ Offer to smoke or have a beverage	❏ Limit chances for further anxiety and say "no thanks."
❏ Meal time interview	❏ Recognize that you are not there to eat; you are there to get a job. Order simply.
❏ Inexperienced, antagonistic, unprepared, or bored interviewer	❏ Be adaptable. Offer clear, concise answers. Read body language to see if you are getting your points across.

☆ 10.1 *What can I do for you?*
Why did you ask to meet with me?

The fact that such a question may come up is one more reason for being sure of your objective for any meeting and for sharing that objective with the person you want to meet with. Before going to any meeting, have a clear idea of the interviewer's role in the selection process and the objective of the meeting. *When this "intimidating" question is asked, there should be no doubt as to the purpose of the meeting.* In appropriate situations, mention directly that you are hoping the person you are meeting with will offer you a job, or at least a "pass-along."

You should do everything you can to avoid the term "informational interview" and also make it a habit to avoid these interviews as well. The informational interview is an opportunity for job applicants to gather data because they have chosen the person to pick his or her brain. What nerve! It becomes even more of a problem when interviewers ask what they can do for you. Does it make sense to say you are only looking for information? If interviewers have a job available, they may not share that fact with you after you claim interest only in gathering information. If you really want a job and say so, then you have lowered your camouflage, and you may make interviewers wonder if they agreed to the interview under false pretenses.

Note: Information interviews are frequently encouraged by outplacement and other career counselors, but they are problematic because they have a confused agenda. Their justification is to stimulate interest in the job seeker and develop a network of contacts with a direct statement up front that this meeting is not to generate a job offer. If anything, the interview should be called a "courtesy" interview instead. What confuses the meeting is the question of who is the interviewer. Job seekers in this instance are really the interviewers because they are interested in obtaining "information," but job holders become the interviewers if they are expected to refer the applicant to others and elsewhere. If it is a courtesy interview, the objective is to extend the courtesy of a meeting, and the conversation determines the next step, if any, by the interviewer (a referral, a direction, a publication).

If you have honestly spoken to the person you are meeting with about the true purpose of the meeting, you might say, for example, *"I was hoping that I would be able to convince you that I am a person your organization would love to hire."*

☆ 10.2 *Can you work overtime? Evenings? Weekends?*
Travel? Entertain at home?

Don't be intimidated. Agree if you are willing to do so. *Take the question or series of questions as opportunities for negotiation.* Don't immediately say yes

without qualification, but seek details and more information first. It is reasonable to ask:

What is overtime like here?

How frequent is it?

Will I get paid for overtime worked [comp time or cash; straight time
and/or time and a half or more]?

For travel, find out the types of location, frequency, and reimbursement
methods.

Watch out for commitments regarding entertainment at home. Consider the details before saying yes. You are perceived as a more knowledgeable person if you do.

Caution: There also may be a hidden illegal agenda. The interviewer
may have determined that you may be of a religious persuasion that prohibits you from working overtime at certain times during the week. This
matter is discussed from that perspective in Chap. 12, "Illegal Questions."

☆ 10.3 Do you have any questions?

A really weak answer is, *"No, because you have already answered them
throughout the interview."* To the interviewer it may sound like, *"I do not
want to be bothered making the effort"* or *"I just want to get out of here."*

Before every interview, as part of the preparation, a list of questions
should be drawn up by the job applicant (for further discussion, see Chap.
13). This preparation accomplishes three objectives:

1. By making this process a habit, job applicants quickly become adept at
   identifying what information they want from every interview.

2. By preparing these questions in advance, no matter when the question
   is popped, applicants are ready to go.

3. By preparing the questions in advance, applicants increase the likelihood that their questions will be answered, but with prepared questions they can truly concentrate on the answers.

10.4 Don't you think you would be better suited to a different sized/type company?

What does this question mean? Most probably, the interviewer has either
written you off or is baiting you. In either instance, *avoid going on the defensive by taking the offensive: "What makes you say that?"* Be careful and try
to take this opportunity to determine what made the interviewer raise the
question in the first place.

In preparation, completing the Job History Worksheet (page 37), My Ideal Job (page 38), Organization Fact Sheet (page 44), and Behavior Worksheet (page 115) should have convinced you that you are interviewing for the right job at the right organization. Now convince the interviewer of the "fit" of your candidacy.

10.5   Have you done the best work you are capable of?

This is a double-edged question. If you say yes, the interviewer may determine that the rest of your career is downhill; if you have already done your best work, only less than that is left. On the other hand, say no and the interviewer wonders why you have done less than your best. To avoid both edges of the sword, answer by saying:

> I have done some terrific things and have had some great accomplishments. This has made me search for greater challenges so that I will be able to even do better work going forward.

10.6   How do you think this interview is going?

Try to stay realistic in your comments. You have nothing to lose because the interviewer is asking your opinion. So you cannot be incorrect. *"I feel uncomfortable in that you do not seem interested in my experience. Am I answering your questions with sufficient detail?"* The worst statement could be the comment that you feel the interview is going well when it is not. Again be sure to seek affirmation from the interviewer. By asking for the interviewer's thoughts at the end of your answer, you get some feedback. Take it.

☆ 10.7   How long have you been looking for a job? Why are you still looking for a job? (Why haven't you found a job yet?)

This stress-building question can easily intimidate you if you have not prepared. Take it for what it is and give it a brief answer. Then be ready for the follow-up inquiry. Be consistent with any other information furnished on your application or resume.

If obviously there has been some length of time since your last job and this has been an undesirable fact of life for you, try to put a positive spin even in the direst of circumstances. Most employers do not want to be faced with a desperate applicant. So try your best to avoid looking like one. Reasons for an extended job search may include:

❑ *"Searching for the right opportunity."* You have not been looking for just another job where you might have to go through this process again after a short period of time.

❑ *"Trying to find a real career opportunity with the right organization."* You have had offers but for one reason or another you preferred to continue the search. If you take this tack, be ready to support it with concrete examples of job offers that you passed up. Do not make the list too long, even if true; two or three examples should always suffice.

❑ *"Personal matters to deal with."* As more and more people are living longer, the working population is more frequently placed in a position of providing assistance to those older than themselves as well as for children. This is true not only for immediate family but for other relatives, neighbors, and friends (including friends of parents) as well. State that you had matters to attend to and, rather than give less than your full attention to your job search, you felt it more appropriate to solve the immediate problem and then give all your energies to the search, which you are now doing.

❑ *"I am completing school."* Have you delayed the completion of your schooling in the past for whatever reason (finances, family, other commitments, such as an obligation to take responsibility for managing the family's business)? Currently more and more people are accepting the fact that the longer ago you left school (completed or not), the less likely it is that the skills you learned are relevant. Cutting-edge thinking now is that education should be a neverending process. By continuing school as an adult throughout your professional life, you are more likely to be current with the latest thinking in your subject areas. Whether the courses are job-related (especially directly) or not, you are perceived as a person interested in personal growth as an ongoing commitment and one who becomes excited by the thrill of the new.

❑ *"Consulting assignments have been keeping me busy."* This is an overused avenue to present. It is as if there is a "universal rule" of nature. Recruiters are always talking about all the out-of-work people who claim they have been consulting while searching for a job. Just as we mentioned with educational pursuits, if this is the route you pursue, make sure you have a complete story because all but the most ill prepared, poorly trained, and least experienced (I think you get the point) interviewers will try to determine the veracity of your portrayal. Be ready not only to have a story but to make it a good one (hopefully truthful) with client profile, perhaps disclosing industry, size, employee numbers, revenues, and/or number of work locations. You don't have to disclose the client's name. By creating a little mystery you are stealing the interviewer's opportunity to evaluate the prestige of your client and to peg you in terms of professional stature. Also, if the interviewer is interested, be ready with a brief summary (very focused and very brief) of the nature of the engagement, including a comment about the result.

❏ *"I am attempting a change in career."* If you mean it, then you have to do some research and lots of homework before you do so. Become focused and determine a plan of action for exploring your chosen path in more depth. You must anticipate booby traps. Is the job or organization you are meeting with consistent with the new career? What activities have you pursued to quickly build up your knowledge in this new area? What about compensation? Do you expect at least to avoid a cut in pay, or is there an apprenticeship aspect that requires paying one's dues? Once you agree to that, though, will the prospective employer anticipate (or hope) that you could be obtained at a cheap price?

If you are contemplating a career change, don't consider yourself odd or an exception. Charles Handy, in his popular book *The Age of Unreason,* says that at the present time people on average go through at least three career changes (not jobs or organizations) in their lifetimes. So we should expect such cases. If you are thinking in these terms, pat yourself on the back because you are considering an action that makes you very contemporary.

❏ *"Your folks called me. I was not looking."* This is a strong response when you have been recruited by a headhunter. This answer puts interviewers on the defensive perhaps because they were not aware of it (and your question now has them weakened because of their lack of information). Or they were aware of it, in which case, why ask the question? Was it to trap the candidate? For shame, particularly now that the ruse has been discovered.

Even if you have been looking for a job for years without success, do not admit it unless you are sure that your unusual approach can generate the response you are looking for. If you admit to a year-long search, the interviewer more often than not questions your abilities and wonders why no one out there is interested in hiring you. There is a very successful fellow with a Ph.D. who took 19 times (by his count) to get hired by the organization that he wanted to work for. If he had disclosed to them just before he was hired that they had already rejected him 18 times, he would never have landed the job. He has already been there for 13 years and continues to move up in the organization.

10.8 How long will it take for you to make a meaningful contribution to our organization?

If you provide too long a time frame, interviewers wonder if you will ever make a contribution. Saying *"From day one!"* requires an explanation of what you can do for the organization immediately. Organizations recognize the learning curve that any new employee is expected to undergo. The *higher the level of the person hired, the more tolerant the organization is about expecting results,* but in those instances the later the impact, the greater the results. In no case extend the time frame beyond six months.

10.9 How fast will you contribute to the organization's success?

This is a variation of the immediately preceding question. It is a little easier to deal with because you can say that you will begin to contribute in small ways from the commencement of your employment. As you grow into your assignment with the organization—and especially after six months—your contributions will grow as well.

10.10 How long would you stay with us?

You need to think right answer/wrong answer for this "gotcha" question. Think about it. If you switched roles with your interviewer, what would you want to hear? Consider the organization you are meeting with and the "time lines" they consider appropriate. If you are meeting with a highly entrepreneurial company, you do not want to say something along the lines of, *"I am looking for a place to stay until I retire."* In most cases, the sedentary and security-tinged tone of the answer will not be well received. Sometimes, however, circumstances can make this answer appropriate even in an entrepreneurial environment. If, for instance, you are nearing retirement age that would be a most effective answer regardless of organization because it tells the employer that there is a specific limit to your stay. At the same time you both know your intent up front.

Consider and try to determine the "right" answer with your interviewer in mind, but be careful not to say something that would reflect inconsistencies with the rest of your presentation. *"I have never been a job hopper. I plan to stay as long as there continue to be challenges."* With that answer, though, be ready for the follow-up: *"What do we have to do to keep you challenged?"* *"As long as I continue to learn"* is a troublesome reply because the tone suggests that the organization is responsible for your well-being and you have now established a problem. The burden on the employer (if they hire you) is to constantly worry that you feel that you are always learning. Employers want applicants who bring solutions with them; they have enough problems already.

In a "paternal" organization, the culture is family-like. That is, you are carefully and constantly oriented to the organization, and the organization tries to do it effectively by blurring the lines between personal and professional. If it is a style you prefer and you see that as the organization's approach, say, *"I plan to stay forever—that is, of course, if the organization permits."* Then explain that you see work as an opportunity to "belong" and that belonging to this great organization would be quite a coup.

☆ 10.11 *How many hours do/did you find it necessary to work each week to get your job done?*

Portray yourself as someone with a strong work ethic but at the same time not overwhelmed by your work, *"It varies"* may be the perfect answer because it allows you next to mention that the usual amount of time you "put in" each week is between 40 and 55 hours. You are then able to add a comment such as that the amount of actual time required depends on a number of factors. If you feel comfortable ending the answer there, it is certainly acceptable.

☆ 10.12 *If our roles were reversed, what questions would you ask?*

If you are ready for this question, usually only one question is required. Ask the question that you feel is most relevant and also affords you the opportunity to give a strong, positive, confident answer. Do not for a second consider a question that comments in any way on your possible inappropriateness for the position and/or organization being discussed. The answer *"You have already covered all the questions very thoroughly"* or something to that effect is weak.

If you feel strong with preparation, suggest either *"What can you do for us?"* or *"What makes you think you want to join our organization?"* These questions tell the interviewer you are a confident person and are willing to answer questions that others may consider intimidating. *This is also a chance to slip in a question that you really want to be asked because you have an excellent response* that can advance your candidacy.

10.13 *Some people feel that spending too much time in any one position shows a lack of initiative. What is your opinion?*

The interviewer may be talking about you. Clarify the point at the beginning of your answer by saying, *"That might be a comment regarding my current job."* Then proceed with the response: *"But I do not think it applies because of the variety of challenges I had to face and grew with—until very recently."* The point is that what constitutes too much time in any position is not a specific length but varies based on the position and the challenges of the position.

10.14   *Have you ever had difficulty getting along with others?*

If your answer presents you in a positive light, then give it as a strong answer.

> *As a matter of fact, yes. I was employed briefly by the U.S. Post Office at its main facility in Boston. I had problems from the start because I wanted to show how productive I could be. Every day, even though I was new, I was setting productivity records. The union steward and then a few of my fellow workers tried to dissuade me by letting me know in very direct language that I was disruptive and my work habits needed to change or I would encounter difficulty in my work relationships. Even my supervisor felt the need to tell me to slow down. I had to leave.*

If you do not have a strong answer like this, just state that you have always found a common ground to deal with others to accomplish the job at hand.

10.15   *What are some of the things that bother/bothered you about your current/last job?*

Preferably identify minor nuisances and inconveniences. Keep in mind that your interviewer is not asking for the purpose of correcting them. Preface your remarks with a comment that, *"For the most part I really liked my job but—as with any job—there were a few minor frustrations."* Then mention irritants that, if corrected, would have enabled you to be more effective. Try to stick with only two.

> *One mail pickup a day.*
> *Overnight delivery packages had to be ready by 5:15.*
> *So many people never checked their e-mail.*

☆ 10.16   *What can I tell you about the organization?*

If this question is asked toward (or at) the beginning of the meeting, it is poorly placed. You need to determine the reason for raising it at such an early point. You need to be ready for it, though, because it happens.

You can let the interviewer know that you wanted to learn more about the organization's current operations (assuming that you have done research already and just need to be brought up-to-date). The only other option is to say something like, *"I have no questions to ask at this time but will save them for later."* Remember that to say something like *"I have no questions"* is perceived as a weak response because a real reason for interviewers to raise the question is to give you the opportunity to show how prepared you are for this meeting. They give you this shot to take the floor because they are not prepared to give you a lot of time and attention if your answer shows that you are not a strong candidate. They feel that their initial impressions have been confirmed and the meeting should be ended as swiftly as possible.

When thinking about what to ask, do not panic. A great open-ended response that is perfectly appropriate here is either, *"How's business?"* or *"How is the company doing?"* Another tactic is to ask the interviewer, *"How long have you been there?"* Then follow up with *"How's business?"* If you have done your research, you can be more specific with questions regarding a new market, product, or location. Be certain of your facts before you open this door.

These can be winning responses because it gets interviewers to talk about themselves. At the same time the question implies that you are evaluating interviewers and that, based on their responses, you will ask additional questions. So the conversation becomes an ever-so-slight test for the interviewer.

Refer to Chap. 13, "Your Turn: Questions You Should Raise," and the index card you prepared in Chap. 4 listing information that you need on the position and/or the organization.

10.17 What can YOU do for us [that someone else cannot]?

You need to briefly give a strong answer. Discuss your skills ("can do") and your motivation ("will do"), relating them specifically to the organization and the position ("fit"). Combine those facts with a comment on your wish to be a part of this organization, and you have given a strong powerful answer.

> *I have not only the technical skill to do all the programming that you require but also a great love for the profession that translates into a strong work ethic. What makes me unique is not only the specific series of experiences that is ideally suited for this environment but my strong interest in becoming a member of this organization.*

☆ 10.18 What do you know about our organization?

Aren't you glad you did research? Do not overwhelm. Sum up briefly the nature and scope of the organization and a brief comment on its age.

I know that you have been a pioneer in the sewage treatment industry and have always led the way since your founding 23 years ago.

10.19 What is the most difficult part of looking for a job for you?

Try this one out before the meeting. To appear effective, your comment might run something like, *"Getting my foot into the door of this organization."* Be alert for any comment that may seem to be whining and do not turn this into a "you-asked-so-I-might-as-well-tell" session. Do not consider interviewers career counselors or therapists (even if they happen to be either). You are there to get a job.

10.20 What outside interests/activities occupy your time?

Included in Chap. 3, "Are You an Open Book?," is a variation of this question. It was worded, *"What do you do in your spare time?"* The variation of that question is included here because there are two aspects to the question. One can be just small talk, trying to find out about you. The other aspect can be related to "fit."

If you are considering a job with a coin collecting company, numismatics would certainly be a related interest. Do not mention too many because you may be perceived as having too many demands on your time already. Consider golf, tennis, and sailing. For example, mention golf if your research confirms that golf is a major corporate pastime, if business is generated with relationships developed during 18 holes of golf, and, above all, *if you already play reasonably well.* Do not under any circumstances pretend to be something you are not because the stakes are not as high. A knowledgeable interviewer could expose you as a charlatan. Why take that risk?

10.21 What question could I ask that would really intimidate you?

This is one of the most terrible questions to deal with because it puts applicants to a test that requires a most demanding answer. Once you state the question, the interviewer then asks the question that he or she would not thought of asking in the first place.

When preparing in advance for this question, consider all the questions that may come up so that this question from the interviewer is just an opportunity to answer another one. The only difference is that the burden is on you not only to provide a question but also to be ready with an answer.

However, there is an alternative: Choose a question that the interviewer has already asked. This accomplishes two things. First, your answer flatters the interviewer, who has already come up with what you consider to be a really intimidating question! Second, by identifying a question already asked, you do not have to answer a tough question that the interviewer had not considered. You do not have to add to the arsenal. Again, you can also take the opportunity to slip in a question for which you have a strong answer.

10.22   What reservations do you have about working here?

If you have any, now is not the time to raise them. Quash the temptation to say something like, "I only hope that I am good enough to make it here." Instead, say:

> *I see this position as a fine opportunity and the organization as one I would be proud to be a member of. I don't have any reservations at this point.*

10.23   What skills or requirements do you think your boss/supervisor should have in this position?

If you know enough about the position to feel qualified to answer, go ahead. In the process, be sure to emphasize the skills and qualities that you possess. If necessary, give a brief mention to other skills that are required and that you may complement or support. Then be silent.

10.24   Where does your boss think you are right now?

This is a nasty question to ask a currently employed applicant. Avoid being caught in a lie:

> *I arranged to take a vacation day/personal day.*
>
> *I rearranged my lunch hour to make this appointment.*
>
> *Since I came in early this morning to clear my desk, I explained to my supervisor that I had a personal matter to attend to this afternoon.*

10.25   Why are you interested in coming to/working in/relocating to [city/town]?

The tone of this question appears negative. To start your answer with that comment may help to determine the interviewer's motivation for the question and feelings toward the place. If you are serious about pursuing a top-level position at Wal-Mart, for example, you need to be very positive about Bentonville, Arkansas. You are not forced to move there. But they do have staff meetings on Saturday mornings, and not only employees but their families are invited to attend.

Regardless of the location, *part of the job search process should include research on the location of the organization facility* where it seems most likely that you will be working. Keep your comments confined to the specific question. Suppose the location is not the most desirable, such as an inner city area ripe for urban renewal or a boring industrial park. Make the point that the reason for your interest in the location is particularly due to the opportunities presented by the organization, which has chosen to set up shop there.

Observe whether the interviewer is not disclosing a bias and is discriminating for whatever reason toward you. You may want to add, *"Please tell me what made you ask the question."* This is an ideal way to get the interviewer to open up without your appearing unnecessarily aggressive.

10.26 Why aren't you earning more at your age?

Another terrible question. Do not succumb. Do not challenge the premise.

When I was just out of college I considered other factors besides pay as being more important. I should have paid more attention to my career in my early years.

That is exactly why we are having this meeting.

☆ 10.27 Why do you want to work for us? Why do you want to work here?

This question, in either format, may be considered discriminatory if asked of minority candidates. The implication is that this place is not for *you* to work. Regardless of your ethnic background, avoid sharing negative comments with interviewers even if they speak disparagingly of the organization.

These are unusual times for organizations. With bitterness sometimes sweeping through downsizing organizations, it is not that rare to run into line managers or personnel/human resource professionals who confide their bitterness. *Listen but do not participate, regardless of your feelings. You are witnessing a bizarre situation.* If you are subjected to a disgruntled employee's monolog during the recruitment and selection process, listen and keep your distance. You may win in two ways. First, a job offer may be coming your way because the person speaking to you liked you enough to open up without fear of—or concern for—retribution. Second, you are getting deep insight into the organization from an insider—great data for you to consider while deciding whether you are interested in joining the organization.

10.28   Would you like to have my job?

Don't be tempted to respond, *"Only for the next ten minutes so that I could hire myself."* Be direct and say, *"With all the challenges in the position I am being considered for, I will certainly be kept busy for quite awhile."*

☆ *10.29   Your resume suggests that you may be over(under)qualified/ too experienced for this position. What do you think?*
You do not seem to have the appropriate experience/education for this position. Why should I hire you?

Interviewers may be letting you know that they have already written you off and they may or may not be giving you one last shot at convincing them otherwise. This question cries out, "You had better show me or else!" Additionally, it may display the true feeling of the interviewer that says, "The clock is ticking and I am running out of patience."

On the other hand, the interviewer may feel that qualifications are not an issue but want to hear it from you. ("Let me be a devil's advocate for a moment....") Either way, treat the question as one that requires "correctness."

Be delicate. You need to strike a balance between agreeing with the person's concerns on the surface and providing a convincing answer that serves to neutralize the concern expressed. One approach may be to start with, *"I certainly appreciate your comment and might agree with your concern.* [Try to avoid using "but" here.] *I wonder whether you have given attention to...."* Avoid using words like "enough" or "ample," which may be considered a criticism and may put interviewers on the defensive because they may feel placed in a position of attack. Once this statement is delivered, a strong positive response must follow. The response should give interviewers the opportunity to easily agree that they did not realize something in your experience, at the same time taking some responsibility for having the interviewer initially thinking otherwise.

> *I am not certain whether I stressed my experience in using both Microsoft Word and Publisher. I have also started to use the other programs found in Microsoft Office to prepare newsletters.*

In a worse case scenario, when interviewers are being kind and you know that you don't have any of the experience that they want, briefly and directly agree with the interviewer. Then move on to a positive statement that indicates your potential.

10.30 *If you were going to Mars, what three things would you take?*

Believe it or not, this question comes up from time to time. One reason may be to challenge your creativity. Another is to determine how you act under pressure. Don't let the question floor you even if it really bothers you. You cannot let the interviewer see that you are easily rattled. Start the answer with a disclaimer: *"I will give the question a shot but please understand that I never took an astronomy course (or it was so long ago that I forgot most of it)."* Then give it a shot. A possible first choice is an expert in the field. Second, sufficient oxygen to allow you to breathe in that environment, and third enough fuel for the return trip.

Two out of the three items chosen show that you are serious about basics, and the expert shows your ability to depend on others who are the experts so that it becomes a team effort. From a seemingly nonsense question, an evaluation may have been extracted by the interviewer.

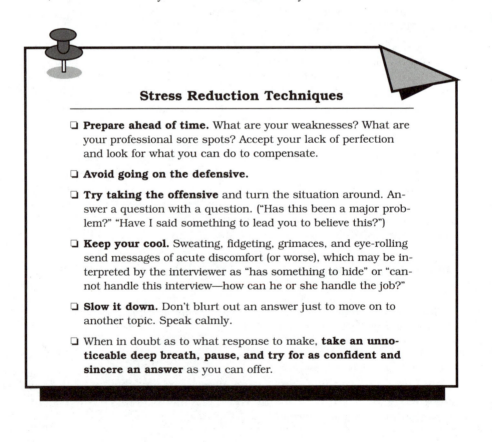

Stress Reduction Techniques

❏ **Prepare ahead of time.** What are your weaknesses? What are your professional sore spots? Accept your lack of perfection and look for what you can do to compensate.

❏ **Avoid going on the defensive.**

❏ **Try taking the offensive** and turn the situation around. Answer a question with a question. ("Has this been a major problem?" "Have I said something to lead you to believe this?")

❏ **Keep your cool.** Sweating, fidgeting, grimaces, and eye-rolling send messages of acute discomfort (or worse), which may be interpreted by the interviewer as "has something to hide" or "cannot handle this interview—how can he or she handle the job?"

❏ **Slow it down.** Don't blurt out an answer just to move on to another topic. Speak calmly.

❏ When in doubt as to what response to make, **take an unnoticeable deep breath, pause, and try for as confident and sincere an answer** as you can offer.

11

Open-Ended and Closed-Ended Questions

How Can You Control the Interview?

The dynamics of interviewing can be exciting to the person who is sensitive to its elements and who has developed an appreciation for them. The person who understands the process is also more effective when serving as a participant. (This goes for interviewers as well as for interviewees.)

Whoever controls the interview has a leg up in the process as long as the person does not make the other person angry while doing it. Some say that the more job applicants get interviewers to do the talking, the greater is the likelihood that they will be successful. People love to hear themselves talk. So it follows that, if interviewers get to do a lot of talking, they feel good about themselves. If they feel good about themselves, they credit the person who is responsible for this feeling.

Does control go to the person in the interview who is talking or to the one who is listening? The astute interviewer recognizes that the listener, with occasional intervention, gets to control the interview. The interviewer with little knowledge of the process or experience more likely considers the opposite to be true.

A major way to control the interview is with the questions. *The person who gets to ask the questions controls the interview, that is, until the other person starts to respond.* If the person who asked the question gives up control, then the person answering has gained control. It is up to questioners to determine whether the answer was given and then, in the spirit of the conversation, talk again. If they raise another question, they have again taken control of the interview.

145

Open-Ended Questions	Closed-Ended Questions
❏ Leave respondents open to answer however they wish. ❏ Respondents can take answer in the direction they choose. ❏ Samples: "How was your trip in this morning?" "Why did you leave your last job?" ❏ Reason asked: More exploratory	❏ Require a yes/no answer. ❏ Samples: "Did you work overtime in your last job?" "Would you like a cup of coffee?" ❏ Reason asked: Ascertain facts in a rapid-fire manner.

We already discussed the topic of small talk, the period at the start-up of the interview that gives the interviewer the opportunity to set the mood. If done correctly, the tone enhances what is to follow because it makes applicants more open to share their thoughts and concerns throughout the rest of the interview.

In this chapter we consider two major categories of questions (open- and closed-ended questions) to see how each type is used to maximize interview effectiveness.

The key to the effectiveness of the process is to be able to go back and forth, using the more appropriate form of question to keep the conversation flowing with the information required to come to a conclusion regarding the applicant's candidacy.

Here is an example of a sequence of questions that an interviewer could use:

❏ **Question 1:** *"Do you work overtime in your present job?"* Notice that it requires the briefest of replies (either "yes," "no," "sometimes," or "depends").

   "Yes."

❏ **Question 2:** *"What causes the overtime to occur?"* Open-ended to give you the option of analyzing the reasons from your experience.

❏ **Question 3:** *"On what basis are the workers chosen to work overtime?"* Another open-ended question that allows you to elaborate.

❏ **Question 4:** *"Did you mind working overtime?"* Getting specific with a closed-ended question leaves you no room to negotiate an answer.

Say that you hated it and the die is cast, depending on the organization's opinion of overtime.

If you say something like, *"Frankly, sometimes it really bothered me"* (a long version of a "yes"), the answer will be pursued with an open-ended question.

❑ **Question 5:** *"Under what circumstances did it bother you?"* This is an effective interview technique using closed-ended questions to focus and open-ended questions to explore the candidate's background.

So What Does This All Mean to You?

Control of the interview belongs to the one who controls the questions. The person providing the answers is following the lead of the questioner. If you consider an interview a dynamic situation, where control flows from one person to the other, you begin to get an idea of the importance of the question mix (open- and closed-ended questions being asked back and forth) as an opportunity to retain control of the interview.

Interviewers are required to obtain answers from your meeting that allow them to conclude accurately the degree of fit between you and the organization. The more interviewers get you to talk, the more likely they are to arrive at an accurate decision based on an effective interview process.

As the applicant, you also want information from the interview. You want first and foremost to be offered a job. You become the interviewer when you try to extract information from employment interviewers so that you may determine whether a job offer, if extended, will be acceptable. The more you learn about the organization, the more able you are to make an informed decision.

For the sake of understanding the dynamics of the interview, therefore, the more you are sensitive to open- and closed-ended questions, the more insight you gain into the effectiveness of interviewers and their competence. If interviewers ask only closed-ended questions, they may be in a hurry—or it might mean something else. The interviewers may be poor interviewers, or they may have no interest. Astute applicants are quickly able to determine a lot about the organization if they understand the intricacies of open- and closed-ended questions.

Note: You never want to upstage interviewers. One way to avoid doing so is to attend to their interviewing style and performance level by meeting them at the competence level they establish.

The Easiest Type of Questions to Answer

The first point to remember is that *closed-ended questions are the easiest to answer because they usually hint at the answer.*

❏ **"Do you work overtime?"** Who needs further analysis before determining the correct answer? *"Of course, I work overtime."*

❏ **"How is your health?"** Everyone is a Cal Ripkin, Jr. *"Never missed a day of work in my life."*

❏ **"We require persons in this position to travel overnight frequently. How do you feel about this requirement?"** *"No problem."*

❏ **"Do you know how to use a SuperZippo PC and its major proprietary software package, Bogus Oats?"** *"Of course."*

Beware of the Follow-up

The astute interviewer follows up with probing questions to see if your answers support your initial answer. After the Bogus Oats question, the interviewer should ask something to determine to what extent you are giving an honest answer. *"Tell me what applications you used Bogus Oats for in your current organization."* Notice that the interviewer used the technical term "applications" to determine your level of PC literacy (or at least its jargon) and at the same time seeks to see what you did with Bogus Oats in your current situation. The applicant cannot answer "yes" or "no," and even more probing is in evidence because you have yet to agree that your familiarity comes from usage in your current organization.

The interviewer has raised a number of issues, and you are at liberty (and have the responsibility) to answer the question in the most appropriate way for you.

Be honest when responding to closed-ended questions, or your bluff may be called. For example, the interviewer could say, *"I am so glad you are familiar with Bogus Oats! I kept getting an error message just before our meeting. Could you look at my screen?"* You thought it was a simple yes/no question, and now you are faced with taking the interviewer's PC on a test drive.

Dry Runs

Identify several skills, experiences, or behaviors that you feel are essential to your candidacy. Then write a scenario with open- and closed-ended questions designed to elicit information from you. For example, if computer literacy is a key issue, the following exchange is likely to occur:

Questions about PC Experience

"What PC do you use at work?" "I use a _____ PC at work."

"What software do you use on a regular basis to accomplish your tasks?"

For each program you identify, provide what output you generate with it.

"Are you responsible for designing reports or only for generating reports that are designed by others?"

"What are your biggest problems with the software you are using?"

"Are there other software packages that would be more effective?"

"What are they and in what way will they be more effective?"

"Do you have a PC at home?"

"What do you use it for?"

Another series of questions could be aimed at your work experience:

Questions about a Team-based Environment

"Here at XYZ Corporation we are a team-based organization. Have you ever worked in a team-based environment?" "Yes."

"In what organization did you work in a team-based environment?"

"Please describe it with details."

"Was it a self-managed work team?"

"If yes, how was the leader chosen?"

"How frequently did the team meet?"

"What issues were discussed at meetings?"

"What problems arose?"

"Did you like working in this environment?"

"What did you like/dislike about that approach to work?"

Questions can end with your answer, or they can
open the door to an entire chain of related questions.
Your answers and the details you provide can either
open or close doors, and it is important that you
consider where the questioning may take you.

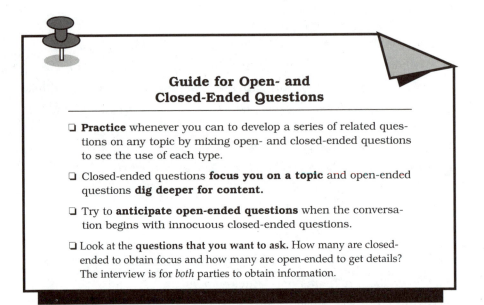

Guide for Open- and Closed-Ended Questions

❏ **Practice** whenever you can to develop a series of related questions on any topic by mixing open- and closed-ended questions to see the use of each type.

❏ Closed-ended questions **focus you on a topic** and open-ended questions **dig deeper for content.**

❏ Try to **anticipate open-ended questions** when the conversation begins with innocuous closed-ended questions.

❏ Look at the **questions that you want to ask.** How many are closed-ended to obtain focus and how many are open-ended to get details? The interview is for *both* parties to obtain information.

12

Illegal Questions

What You Shouldn't Have to Answer
(But May Have To)

For those of us living in the United States or Canada and born under the common law concepts and traditions of medieval England, government protection in the workplace stems primarily from common law practices and traditions that go back to medieval times and to a primarily agricultural society.

The *employment at will principle* is a major common law standard in this tradition. Briefly it says that *an offer to work (from an employer) and an agreement to provide services (by an employee) is based on a voluntary agreement (or contract) by both parties.* Unless otherwise stated by contractual wording, the agreement may be entered into for a good reason, a bad reason, or no reason at all, and may be terminated the same way—upon notice to either party. In this agreement the principle tries to emphasize the fact that the agreement is between two independent parties and that the power of each is "equal."

However, as we know, employers more often than not hold the upper hand because there are usually more applicants than jobs available. So the employer, more often than not, hires and terminates for a good reason, a bad reason, or no reason at all. And, as already stated, this can be done without notice.

Traditionally, employers in this country conducted the selection process in precisely that manner, and the federal government did not interfere until the passage of civil rights legislation in the 1960s. (Federal legislation had been passed earlier that protected the rights of workers who were union members or who had union sympathies—under certain circumstances.)

The first law passed was the Equal Pay Act of 1963. This law protects women—and men—against gender-based pay decisions. In simple English, the law prohibits basing wage and salary decisions on whether the person being paid is a man or a woman. The primary beneficiaries were seen to be women because at the time studies conducted showed consistently that women were paid significantly lower rates than men for the same jobs.

The Civil Rights Act of 1964 was intended to protect the civil rights of all people and prohibited discrimination based on the following characteristics: race, creed, color, national origin, and sex. Title Seven of the Civil Rights Act of 1964 specifically prohibits discrimination in any of the terms and conditions of employment (including, of course, hiring and firing). What effect, if any, did the Civil Rights Act of 1964 have on the common law principle of employment at will? **Employers are still entitled to make decisions regarding the terms and conditions of employment (including hiring decisions) for "a good reason, a bad reason, or no reason at all," provided that they do not violate the provisions of the Civil Rights Act of 1964 or of any subsequent legislation.**

Other federal laws that deal with private sector workplace discrimination issues include:

Americans with Disabilities Act.

Vietnam Era Veterans' Readjustment Act.

Federal Pregnancy Act.

Age Discrimination in Employment Act.

A variety of antidiscrimination laws at the state and municipal levels also protect same-sex partners and make sexual preference or orientation a protected category.

What about Affirmative Action?

Affirmative action has been important since the sixties. In 1966, President Lyndon B. Johnson initiated action to create Executive Order 11246 which not only prohibits, under certain conditions, contractors of the federal government from discriminating against any applicants or employees in any terms and condition of employment with regard to race, color, creed, national origin, or sex, but also requires employers with 50 or more employees to take affirmative steps to correct past imbalances. *Remember two aspects about this policy: First, this is not a law; it is an executive order. Second, organizations that are not federal contractors do not have to enforce it.* There are organizations however, that are not federal contractors but have determined that affirmative action is good business policy. They have voluntarily adopted affirmative action steps to create a more diverse organization.

Affirmative action has been accused of introducing quotas to the workplace. Yet all the related guidelines and interpretations are supposed to be considered targets and guidelines. They are not to be rigidly enforced or adhered to to the extent that a quota is firmly established. To do so is to go beyond what affirmative action is intended to do and to raise other discrimination issues (for example, reverse discrimination).

When applying for a job, applicants should be current in their knowledge about the various employment laws, if affected by them. Persons applying for jobs who have disabilities should know, for instance, that the Americans with Disabilities Act prohibits employers from discriminating against persons with disabilities and requires reasonable accommodations to be made but does not require any affirmative action steps.

Can Employers Still Discriminate? Yes

A widely accepted misconception is that, due to the antidiscrimination laws, employers may no longer discriminate in the workplace. This is not true, and the selection process (as well as, in fact, the recruitment process) is by its nature discriminatory: Applicants are "discriminated out" and others are "discriminated in." The most discriminatory step of all occurs when the selection decision is made, because only one person is hired. All the rest are rejected. **The decision to hire one person discriminates against all the other applicants.**

What an employer *may not do* is discriminate against employees and applicants on the basis of any category protected by law. Employers may still ask irrelevant (to the applicant) questions as long as they do not touch on categories defined and protected by this law.

For example, an employer who distrusts people who wear green socks may be prompted to ask, upon noticing that the applicant is not wearing green socks, "If you were employed here, would you wear green socks?" It is perfectly legal (absurd though it may be from a business perspective), under the common law principle, to refuse to hire applicants who say they would wear green socks, if the employer makes that a term and condition of employment.

There may be valid business reasons for what at first appear to be strange reasons for job consideration. For example, if you are being considered for a job at a fragrance company and you went to the interview wearing a competitor's fragrance, the interviewer can reject you for your poor judgment in fragrance. This becomes more of an issue the higher you rise on the organizational ladder. If you are interviewing for a vice-president's position, the "mistake" (as interpreted by the interviewer) might be much more noticeable by the interviewing organization than if you were applying for a position as an entry-level clerk.

You may think certain questions are illegal that are not. Users of tobacco products (smoke or smokeless) may be discriminated against, as may be persons who are extremely tall or short. Facial hair (or the lack of it) may also be grounds for rejection, as can be rings (ear, tongue, or belly, for example), whistleblowing, and extramarital relationships.

What Is an Illegal Question?

The most obvious illegal questions are those that *directly address characteristics of the person that are protected by law and that are not required to be answered for a determination of the person's eligibility.*

12.1   Where were you born?

This is a most obvious example of a blatantly illegal question. More subtle but just as illegal is another form: *"That is an interesting accent. Where are you from?"* Title VII of the Civil Rights Act of 1964 prohibits discrimination on the basis of national origin. If interviewers ask the question, they are asking for a reason. If the purpose of the meeting is to consider an applicant for the job, then the answer influences, if not determines, the interviewer's conclusion.

Other patently illegal questions are:

> *What religion do you practice?*
> *I see that we live in the same community. I've never seen you at temple. Where do you go?*

Under certain unique circumstances, such questions may be considered appropriate. See the discussion of bona fide occupational qualifications (BFOQ).

An Exception to Remember—BFOQ's

An otherwise illegal line of inquiry may be construed as legal under certain specific circumstances. State and local laws may be even more stringent. Local laws, for instance, may even have a sexual orientation prohibition as well. So consider the community where the employer is located. *These laws specifically permit discrimination for the specific organization if the unique need of the job requires it.* For instance:

- ❏ If the employer is in the catalog business and needs a model for children's, men's, or women's clothes, only then may the employer legally consider the gender and or age of the applicants and include the requirement in advertisements.

- ❏ A church, synagogue, or temple still has the right to insist that persons hired to fulfill the religious aspects of any open position (for example, priest or rabbi) be practicing members of the same religion.

A prominent labor attorney, Harry Rissetto, has insisted that only one occupation will always be a bona fide occupational qualification (BFOQ) and will be the only one to stand the test of time and that is a wet nurse.

Difference between Illegal and Inappropriate Questions

12.2 Are you married?

This is a gray area question. On the face of it, it *may not be illegal to ask the question, provided that you ask it of both men and women applicants and there is no state or local law that protects applicants from discrimination based on marital status.*

On the other hand, the question is terrible because it may raise legal issues and, once a complaint is filed, the burden of proof rests with the employer. Interviewers may be extremely objective and careful to conduct highly structured interviews, but the complaining applicant probably doesn't know it.

12.3 Do you have any children?
Do you plan to have children?
Who cares for your children while you work?

Again, such questions are not truly illegal and may be asked if asked of all applicants (male and female, married and unmarried). But what is the purpose of the question? It is certainly one that may cause annoyed applicants to file complaints because they do not know (even if the interviewers say so) that the practice is to ask every applicant the question. Who needs a complaint filed?

If you are asking this question because you would like to learn more about my commitment to my career, let me assure you that the time I have spent building my career and the drive I have to work will not be replaced with domestic issues.

If you are asking because you are concerned about "coverage," I have very reliable primary and secondary child care coverage. I assure you that I will not be distracted from my work because of child care issues. When you discuss my performance with my references, you will learn that even overnight travel is never a problem.

Why Do Employer Representatives Ask Illegal Questions?

❏ **They may be asked out of ignorance.** The person asking may be a U.S. citizen with little or no experience abroad for personal or professional reasons. On the other hand, the interviewer may be from another country on assignment here. In the United States today many people come to our shores on assignment from their organizations headquartered overseas. In other countries (and even in international agencies located in the United States that continue to be behind the times), questions that are forbidden here are part of the process elsewhere. Questions regarding age, marital status, and family are taken for granted and are a demonstration of the organization's interest in the whole person.

❏ **They may be asked out of arrogance.** A certain strange group of people try to raise illegal issues. For odd reasons they feel the need to test authority. They are going to ask anything they "damn well please," and no human resource professional and, for that matter, no one else is going to stop them. To make their point, persons with this attitude take any recruitment and selection opportunity to ask illegal and other inappropriate questions. They may do it for shock value or because they wish to intimidate, but they do it and anyone looking for a job needs to be prepared for them and their questions.

❏ **They may be asked out of innocence.** Poor interviewers are those who have had little or no training. They may even have the training and/or experience, but they do not have the proficiency required to interview effectively. The problem may also stem from the mere fact that they had no or little time to prepare for the interview. Whatever the reason, these persons frequently try to impress themselves with the ease with which they are able to ask questions. Yet they do not realize that the key to effective interviewing is not thinking about the next question but rather concentrating on the answers. As a result, when these persons realize that they have run out of questions but feel they are not ready to close the meeting, they blurt out an illegal question (*"Are you married?"*) or a high-risk one (*"Do you have any children?"*). These interviewers may be intimidated by the applicant and seek to find common ground (children of the same ages, similar religions) in an effort to put themselves more at ease.

What to Say When Asked an Illegal or Inappropriate Question

First of all, you may consider answering the question and getting on with the interview. You may also consider not answering the question by stating, *"You are asking a question of doubtful legality, and I will not subject myself to this line of questioning."*

What about the worst case scenario? What if the interviewer persists with the illegal questions? If interviewers ask you an illegal question, always remember the first and most important rule: Do not take it personally. This is not to say that you should excuse it or treat it lightly. The point is that, if the question is being asked of you, it has probably been asked of who knows how many others. These interviewers are continuing to ask illegal questions because they have not been confronted with a refusal to answer. They may have a number of reasons for pursuing this line of inquiry, as discussed in this chapter. If they continue to ask what you perceive to be one or more illegal questions, you may attempt to address the issue firmly but diplomatically by repeating your response. If they still continue, their message is one of either total ignorance of the law or complete disregard for it. It is to be hoped that you will never have to face this type of encounter. If you do, no matter how desperate you are for a job, remember that the job offer will more than likely never come anyway. So my suggestion is to terminate the interview and make the decision whether to file a complaint.

Gender Bias Questions

Unfortunately, bias remains in the workplace, and tainted or illegal questions are usually asked of women.

12.4 *Are you married? Are you single, married, or divorced?*

I am not sure of your purpose in asking the question. If it is because you are worried about the amount of time I will devote to my work, let me assure you that my first commitment will be to this organization. With every job I have held, my first commitment has always been to my employer. The same would be true if you hired me.

The interviewer may not be as blatant in framing the questions. *The interviewer may be "fishing" to determine your marital status* by offering instead:

Do you prefer to be called Miss, Mrs. or Ms.?
What was your maiden name?

You can avoid the first question by suggesting the use of a first name instead. If the interviewer persists, ask what the custom is in the organization. If there is no custom or you are pressured to make a choice, go with your instinct. Regardless of whether interviewers give you a reason, if you feel they are really persistent and require an answer and will not be put off, consider Ms. If they feel (and this is likely a "he") that they need to know, "Ms." puts them on alert. If you lose the opportunity for any possibility of a job, look on the rejection as a blessing because of the atmosphere in the organization as reflected by the actions of the interviewer.

The question *"What is your maiden name?"* is really about your marital status. The legal way to ask the question is to ask on the application and not in the interview: *"Have you ever used any other names? If so, give them and briefly describe the circumstances."* If the question is asked outright in the interview, counter with, *"I assume that you are seeking this answer because you are going to perform a reference check. My entire professional life has been under my current name."*

12.5   This job requires long hours. Will this be a problem for your spouse and/or your children?

My job is an important part of my life. My family realizes and appreciates that fact and are very flexible with my schedule. When you check my references [if this is so], you will see that my record and credibility attest to that standard of performance.

12.6   Where does your spouse work?

The answer allows interviewers to learn whether you are married. Other insights may be gleaned from your answer without asking. If your spouse does not work, interviewers know that you are the sole support and that there may be children or other dependents to inquire about. If your spouse is working, interviewers have an opportunity to peg the applicant in status both by where the spouse works and what the spouse does. (This is a follow-up question or one that might not even need to be asked, if the applicant wishes to disclose.) Additionally, if interviewers learn that your spouse works, then a follow-up question is who takes care of the kids if they need care during scheduled work hours. This is a particularly interesting and important question if the applicant is interviewing for a job that requires any overnight travel. Interviewers, when not direct, get into trouble with illegal questions. With the increasing numbers of single parents and two-career families, organizations are—and should be—rightfully concerned about outside commitments and coverage. To stay in legal territory they should mention their concern to all applicants—male and female—to get the answers they need.

12.7 *Whom should we notify in case of emergency?*

This question still sometimes appears on application forms. *The question is inappropriate to ask before the person is hired.* It may be asked just because "it has always been there" or because interviewers are probing for information that they may not otherwise be able to obtain. They are hoping you will name your spouse. Not only do interviewers learn that you are married without asking, but they also get a workplace telephone number, thereby discovering what your spouse does for a living or whether he or she works at all. If the question appears on the application form, you may leave it blank. Most people reviewing your application do not even notice. If it comes up, say, *"I didn't bring a workplace number with me but I will get it for you."* Don't mention the workplace number of whom by name or relationship. Chances are that will be the end of the inquiry. If it isn't, ask the reason for the persistence now, and apologize one more time for the information not being available. Then leave it at that.

12.8 *If you were offered this job and accepted, you would be required to work with a mostly male [and/or Hispanic or born-again Christian or any other identifiable group] staff. Would this represent a potential problem for you?*

This is asked generally of women applying for a job in a traditional male area but it may also be asked of men in an area traditionally occupied by women.

No, in my profession, I am expected to deal with a lot of men [women]. I have experience dealing with a variety of people. I have always managed to build credibility and respect. I have created a positive working environment for every member of the team.

None at all. The key to an effective working environment is to establish performance standards and then make sure that each person on the team understands them. Each team member would realize that they will be evaluated by their adherence to those standards. To be effective, the team needs to universally accept basic standards regardless of their backgrounds or experience. Once this is communicated, then each member of the team has a standard to meet and a team to do it with. This becomes a major benchmark for growing the team because it is more important than perceived differences.

12.9 I see that when you worked you frequently changed jobs. What would make your stay here different?

Due to unusual personal circumstances, I have had to make adjustments and changes in the past. Now, however, circumstances have changed [if they have] and I am more able to concentrate on my career and my work.

12.10 You haven't worked in years. What makes you think you are up to the challenges of the position and our organization?

While I have not worked as an employee earning a paycheck for several years, I have had to perform a variety of activities and play a number of roles for projects in the _____ sector. Let me give you an example of skills that I have developed that I am certain will be most useful to you here. For example, I supervised the automation of the XYZ Agency [Association] that brought the organization into the information age and did it while expanding fundraising efforts.

Do not say, "… and I was able to obtain all the equipment for free." This cuts down on the mystique by providing too much information and may conjure up visions of your taking possession of all this discarded equipment.

National Origin Questions

12.11 That is an interesting accent. What country are you from?
What country are your parents from?
You have an unusual last name. Where do you come from?

Other variations may include:

What is your native language?

What language do you speak at home?

I see on your resume you mention that you are fluent in _____. How did you have the opportunity to learn that language?

Are you from China or Korea [or Africa or the Caribbean]?
Where were you born?
You are a citizen of what country?

Interviewers may raise such questions either because they have run out of questions or because they are truly curious. You may wait for them to make an additional comment to indicate how the question is job-relevant (you are being considered for an overseas post, for instance). You may certainly ask, *"Are you concerned that my birthplace has some bearing on how I will perform if hired by you?"* Or you can say something to engage and redirect the interviewer by talking about someplace you might have visited for a time. The most direct response is to let the interviewer know that you have a problem with the question. Go on to mention that you wonder whether the question indicates a negative judgment on the interviewer's part and therefore might eliminate you from further consideration and terminate the interview.

These inquiries are by their very nature against the law unless there are specific BFOQ reasons for asking them. Employers tend to be careless and frequently poorly prepared for the interviews. BFOQs are becoming more and more rare. Fluency in the German language may be a BFOQ requirement for a German bank doing business in Chicago, but German citizenship or birth is not.

12.12   *What do your parents do?*

This question is raised by interviewers who are interested in determining whether the applicant comes from a home background that is in some way related to the work habits that this organization *thinks* it requires. Even though this is certainly an interesting question for a biographer, it is not job-relevant. Would it be a positive or negative to be in a prominent family whose founders had created an empire or a dynasty? Should it be held against (or in favor of) the applicant if this is so? To make the point more obvious, consider the following: More and more Americans are going to jail. To make matters worse, in some communities it is a status symbol for a family member to be in jail. If that fact were to come from a discussion regarding this question, how would the interviewer respond?

How do you answer this question? *Do not share more information than required and try not to share your annoyance.* For example, if your mother was a widow:

My father worked hard his whole life but he passed away _____ years ago (if this is true). Is there something else you seek on this subject that I could help you with?

State briefly what occupation your father had that you last knew. If you don't know what your parent did, don't mention it. Say instead that your parents separated at an early age and your father, mother, or other relative raised you.

However, *if a parent had a positive tie-in to the organization or industry that you are seeking employment with, you may want to mention this fact.*

> *My mother is a marketing analyst and she has always pointed out to me your innovative advertising campaigns.*
>
> *My father ran a gym and took me to wrestling matches since I was five years old. I recognized quite of few of the Superstars featured in the photos in your lobby.*

12.13   Do you think you will have a problem working in a department that is predominantly white [or black, or Asian, or another ethnic group]?

On the face of it, this is not an illegal question. Yet it has undertones of bias and is a question that may be asked of anyone who is different from the predominant ethnic, race, or national origin characteristic of the work group. The question is intended to determine whether applicants will fit in the work group. Look into your background for examples to cite your effectiveness with diverse work groups.

> *I am confident that I will be an effective member of the work team. In the past I have had experience working with _____, and my record shows my effectiveness in performing successfully in that environment. For example, at XYZ Organization, the work team was comprised of _____ and we increased production by _____ [or some other meaningful statistic], while I was there.*

Questions Suggesting Religious Bias

12.14   Are you a religious person? What denomination?

This question is never appropriate with a very singular exception. For those seeking a life as religious professionals—priests, nuns, rabbis, ministers, or teachers in a religious school (although here the grounds are shaky legally) where belief is still considered a BFOQ—the question may be asked. Even if you are seeking a job in a religious-affiliated institution, it is quite possible that your beliefs or disbeliefs may not even then be the subject of inquiry during the application process.

12.15 Will you have to take time off for any religious holidays? Can you work late on Fridays? Can you come in on Saturdays or Sundays for special projects? We sometimes work overtime weekends. Will this be a problem for you?

On what basis is the subject raised? Have you chosen to disclose your religious beliefs on the application or on any other documentation? Is it due to your attire? Is the interviewer's assumption accurate? Regardless of its basis, the phrasing of the question is still not appropriate. If the interviewer has a concern, then specifics must be provided by the organization in terms of what may be required in the department you are applying for.

If there is no conflict with the duties and hours, say so. If there is a conflict or the potential for future conflicts, you should determine in advance the nature and degree of your commitment to your religion. If there are one or two days (or one or two weeks) a year that you absolutely need off, say so. However, do so in a way that demonstrates that you will be willing to do whatever you can to reasonably accommodate the employer's requirements and work load (even though the guidelines and court decisions say the burden is on the employer to make reasonable accommodations). By your suggesting ways to do it (using vacation entitlement, for instance), you show employers that you are looking to work with them to find a solution. Do not choose to place the burden on employers by saying, in so many words, *"The law says you must accommodate me; so don't bug me or I will take you to court."* Instead:

> *If there is not enough time during the workweek to complete the task assigned, I will certainly work with your supervisor to complete the task however I can. If that requires weekend work, if I am unable to work Sunday [or Saturday], there is no problem with working the other day.*

12.16 I noticed that you did not shake my hand when I offered it. Is there a religious reason why you chose not to do so?

If the answer is yes, answer this question in a matter-of-fact way. *"Yes, the only reason is religious. I certainly intended no ill will."* If there is another reason (for example, you do not like to touch other people because they all carry germs), say so briefly and succinctly, if you wish. But don't show yourself to be a fanatic over the cause.

12.17 What organizations do you belong to?

Regardless of the intent of the inquirer (the term "inquisitor" almost seems appropriate), remember that you are the one giving information. Disclose only what you wish. If you want to show professional expertise, give an organization or two that is particularly appropriate for your profession. Be careful not to fudge here or on your resume. Make sure that you have the completely accurate current organizational name. There is nothing more embarrassing than to identify yourself as a member of XYZ Organization only to learn that the name changed four years ago to ABCD.

Age Bias Questions

12.18   How old are you?

Consider this an opportunity to take the offensive but do not gloat. You could be humorous or nasty:

> *Old enough to know I want to work here.*
> *Young enough to enjoy every day.*

Plan instead either to give the answer and wait for the next question, or, if you feel you do not want to disclose your age, to withhold that information. You cannot take both approaches.

A third approach is to lie. In this area, I have no problem telling you that, if you feel strongly about this issue, you have no reason to disclose your true age. If you are fit and look much younger than you appear, give the age that you feel you appear to be (perhaps even one or two years less). If you are in terrible shape, have had a tough life, and look older than you are, it may be to your advantage to say so.

Whichever approach you take, after you give your answer, be absolutely quiet and wait for the interviewer to say something. Do not break the silence regardless of how long it lasts. The longer it takes for the interviewer to say anything after your answer, the more of an advantage you have. Do not break the silence, even if it takes forever (or what seems like forever).

12.19   Can you read well enough to take this test?

This question deserves a quizzical look as a practical nonverbal response. If you are not able to give one effectively (or camouflage your anger with a poker face), swallow your desire to retort, *"Now what do you mean by that?"* Be nonplussed and state in very even tones instead, *"I am sure I can."*

12.20   Change drives this organization. How flexible are you? How do you deal with change?

This may be a nonbiased question that is asked of everyone in a dynamic, constantly changing environment. It may also be reserved for those who seem too old to be flexible or competent. One of the most biased folk sayings in this country is the terrible one about not being able to teach an old dog new tricks. Be brief, direct, and focused with your answer.

I am very accustomed to change. My last position certainly is an indication of how I thrive in a changing environment. Let me give you a brief example.

12.21   Don't you think you are a little young to be seeking this position?

This is an obvious age bias question that discriminates against youth.

If you only looked at my birth date I might agree with you, but if you look at my resume you will see that I worked throughout college in this industry as a _____. Since that was when our technology was in its infancy, I have literally grown up with the industry.

12.22   Would you be willing to start at a lower salary level because of your inexperience?

Watch carefully for this one. There may be a hidden agenda here because women and minorities frequently are paid less for the position than men. Think ahead for your answer to this one. *Ask what the range of the position is.* Recognize that a premium is to be paid for those who show more expertise, and one way to do that is through demonstrated experience. If the organization has wage and salary ranges, interviewers may or may not share that information with you. Even if they do not, you show your sophistication by asking the question.

I appreciate that salary may be commensurate with experience and that I may command less. That is acceptable as long as the salary is within the range for the position. I am very interested in working for the organization and am confident that my performance will allow salary increases according to the organization's policy.

12.23   What kind of discharge did you receive from the military?

This question is more likely to be carried over from previous versions of the employment application and is really not to be asked. If it appears on the application and you prefer to leave it blank, do so. If you feel better addressing this issue in preparation for the job search, contact the Veterans Administration prior to your job search to determine whether there has been any change in the status of your discharge. If there has not been, can anything be done to change that status so that it looks better whenever an employer asks the question?

Questions Addressing
the Disabled

12.24 *Are you disabled? Are you handicapped?*
How did you become disabled?
How long have you been disabled?
How severe is your disability?

These sweeping questions are not directly job related and are not permissible under the guidelines established by the Americans with Disabilities Act. Interviewers may specifically ask about a disability that might prevent you from performing the job for which you are applying without some accommodation, but they may not pose the question in any of these ways. If you have a disability that is not readily apparent, to be protected by the law you must indicate that you are disabled (isn't that a catch-22 for disclosure?).

The question about the circumstances and/or time that you have been disabled is not related directly to job performance. These issues are history and therefore may prejudice the interviewer. There was, as an example, a quadriplegic who suffered a spinal cord injury that left him disabled from the waist down as the result of a gunshot wound in a gun battle that raged around him while he was an innocent observer. Because it was a gunshot wound, unfair assumptions were made about his lifestyle and morals, and he suffered discrimination while seeking employment.

Other Illegal Questions

12.25 *Have you ever filed a workers' compensation claim?*

It is against the Workers' Compensation Laws to withhold a job from an applicant because of prior workers' compensation claims. *To ask the question is on its face completely illegal and there is no excuse for asking it.* You can confront the interviewer and say that the question is illegal. You can say, *"I do not have to answer the question."* Interviewers may not be pleased with the exchange and will probably also assume that you have had claims— or else you would not make an issue of the question. Or, since they had no right to ask the question, you then have no responsibility to be truthful; you can just say no and be quiet. If lying is offensive, even though the question is inappropriate, then be truthful and give a brief comment especially if it was a minor claim. It is best, however, not to mention it in the first place.

12.26 *Have you ever been a target (or victim) of sexual harassment? Have you ever filed a sexual harassment (or any other EEO or human rights) complaint?*

These questions are raised to determine your proclivity to take legal action in the workplace. The primary issue is whether employers have the right to ask such questions. My opinion is that because they do, you should beware of your answer. To say that you have filed suits raises questions about whether employers will face the same problems with you as an employee. Whether or not justice was on your side, discussing the problem only raises doubt and uncertainty in the minds of most interviewers—regardless of whether they possess the same EEO-protected characteristics as the applicant.

12.27 *Has a sexual harassment complaint ever been filed against you? Have you ever been found guilty of sexual harassment?*

This question was discussed in a slightly different format earlier (see page 33). This is a tough one because, *once the question is raised, you need to answer honestly.* Be careful from the point of view of self-incrimination. However, if there was an investigation and no cause was found, take the view that the complaint was without merit. Because it was ultimately withdrawn, give an answer based on the ultimate determination and not the initiation.

On the other hand, if the question is raised and you were found guilty of sexual harassment, admit it and state the circumstances. Mention that the consequences you had to deal with will demonstrate that you will never be accused again (if that is the way you truly feel). To deny the situation is to promote an application with a lie. If and when the truth is uncovered, termination and humiliation could follow. Some employers accept the fact if the applicant is honest and up front. The alternative is to create a false impression and take the risk that sooner or later the word (and rumors) will spread—even if the case did not make it to the media.

Whistleblowing

If your employer was engaged in what you perceived to be illegal or unethical practices, and you called a government agency or other organization (for example, the newspapers, environmental groups) to alert them, you may end up without a job. Frequently, there is nothing illegal about such a termination. If you are meeting with an employer who has a great and squeaky clean reputation, you may find a receptive ear for what you were trying to accomplish with your last employer. Even then, I would pause to consider the pluses and minuses of disclosure. You are taking a real risk. Is it worth it?

12.28 Have you ever been arrested?

This question is not to be asked. In this country, a person who is arrested is innocent until proven guilty. If there is any line of inquiry that should be pursued by the employer, it is to discover whether the applicant has ever been *convicted* of a crime. If the arrest question is asked, usually on an application form, and you have not been convicted, I would answer the question as if the word *convicted* appeared instead and act accordingly. It really is a breach of trust and illegal to probe into a person's arrest record and not pay attention to convictions.

12.29 My kids are always sick with colds and flu. How about yours?

This is an interesting way to ask a question with innuendo. First, if the question is the first to address the issue of children and dependents, it may also be a subtle way to determine whether you have any. Second, the question may be raised to learn whether you will frequently be out of work. Third, the question may be used to anticipate whether your presence in the organization will translate into high utilization of the organization's medical plan.

If you have no kids, say so and be quiet. If you have kids and feel you can honestly say it, mention you have been fortunate that your kids have always been healthy. Add that you have always been prepared, however, for sickness and injury coverage because you realize the importance of planning and preparedness in that area. If you have someone either nearby or living with you who would be the primary care provider, mention it. Your answer is stronger (and demonstrates your professional approach to your personal commitments) if you mention this person, but including it is not necessary.

Do not under any circumstances disclose too much in terms of a list of recent illnesses or injuries, even if you feel it is a light topic because now all the crises have passed. You are lingering on the topic and probably coming across as verbose. You may be perceived as someone who has been burdened with a difficult family situation.

12.30   *We have a great medical plan. Did you get stuck with a lot of bills last year?*

It doesn't take a rocket scientist to determine the probable reason for asking this question. Even if that was not the intent of the interviewer, now is not the time to find out. There is no reason to disclose your personal situation. So don't do it regardless of the level of temptation. For the most honest, let me add that, even if last year was the worst ever, the medical costs can always be greater. So even in this situation you certainly may honestly say no. What may be "a lot" to one family may be nothing to another.

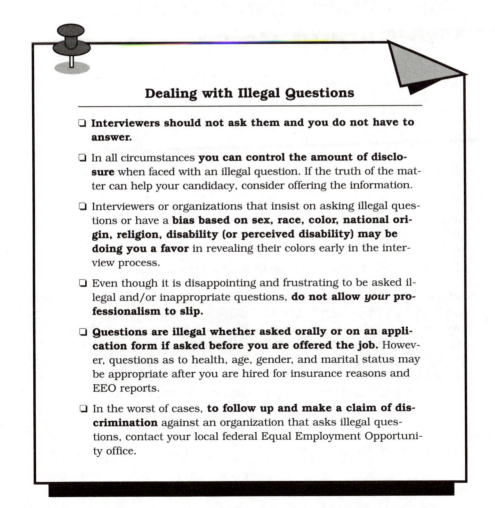

Dealing with Illegal Questions

❑ **Interviewers should not ask them and you do not have to answer.**

❑ In all circumstances **you can control the amount of disclosure** when faced with an illegal question. If the truth of the matter can help your candidacy, consider offering the information.

❑ Interviewers or organizations that insist on asking illegal questions or have a **bias based on sex, race, color, national origin, religion, disability (or perceived disability) may be doing you a favor** in revealing their colors early in the interview process.

❑ Even though it is disappointing and frustrating to be asked illegal and/or inappropriate questions, **do not allow *your* professionalism to slip.**

❑ **Questions are illegal whether asked orally or on an application form if asked before you are offered the job.** However, questions as to health, age, gender, and marital status may be appropriate after you are hired for insurance reasons and EEO reports.

❑ In the worst of cases, **to follow up and make a claim of discrimination** against an organization that asks illegal questions, contact your local federal Equal Employment Opportunity office.

13

Your Turn: Questions You Should Raise

What Should You Know Before the Interview Is Over?

Since an interview is a conversation with a purpose, not a monolog, applicants, as contraparties in the conversation, may ask questions also. If they do not ask questions, they have "failed" their part of the interview because interviewers feel that the applicant:

❑ Is not sufficiently interested to raise questions.

❑ Does not have enough information or experience to raise them.

Questions that applicants are expected to ask during the interview are important. In effect, applicants who don't ask questions can score all the right answers to the questions posed but leave interviewers in doubt as to their level of interest. This is not to say that you must ask a question—any question—in order to "pass." On the contrary, if the give and take during the interview was ideal, all (or at least most) of your questions should have been asked and answered at some time during the process.

Before the Interview

Before the meeting, while doing your research, you probably have many questions that remain unanswered. Getting ready for any employment interview should include the preparation of *questions that* you *need answered to decide in order to accept an offer.* Starting out with questions to have answered goes back to the one original question: *"What is the purpose of this interview?"* Is it to be offered a job? If so, what information do you need to make a decision if the job is offered? Do not forget that the organization must "sell" itself to you during the interview. If you are too concerned with giving information, you may find yourself left out of the loop when it comes to deciding if you want the job if it is offered because you lack details for making your decision.

During the Interview

Your questions should be written down before the meeting. But what do you do with that sheet of paper during the interview? Show it or not? What about reading your questions from a sheet of paper and taking notes during the interview? I suggest you keep it to yourself since it may prove to be a distraction or suggest to the interviewer that you are not sufficiently organized to remember what you want to know.

In this society *it is not considered appropriate to take notes during an employment interview.* Our society is so litigious that tape recorders and note taking by any other form (such as paper and pencil) are considered threats. That said, how do you remember the answers to the questions you raised? You should debrief yourself immediately after each and every interview (refer to Chap. 14, Interview Follow-Up Worksheet, page 176). The primary reason is that we all forget more than 60 percent of anything we have been told within three days after hearing it. The sooner after the meeting you review the answers, the better the chance you have of retaining the correct answers.

Pitfalls and Risks

Does raising certain questions put you at risk? When you ask questions, you are still providing "answers" and information to the interviewer. So, yes, there can be a risk. *The burden is on you to determine* **what question to ask, how to ask it,** *and, most importantly,* **when.** Keep in mind that "the best answers are those given to the questions not asked." Every question you do not have to ask is one less to be worried about asking.

In addition to asking an inappropriate question, there is always the risk that the question is a good one but its timing is off. For example *"What benefits are offered to employees here at XYZ organization?"* If you ask this question during the first few moments of your first interview, you will probably never need to know the answer. The interviewer is most likely to consider you more interested in benefits than the job or the organization.

On the other hand, if the question is asked at the very end of the recruitment process, the moment is appropriate. The issue should be discussed before the offer is made so that the applicant may have the opportunity to obtain information to make a decision about joining the organization.

One last word of caution: Beware of pitfalls when raising questions. If you were articulate when providing answers, now you need all the more to be careful about the questions. Asking a question that is inappropriate or that the interviewer does not even have the answer for may pose problems sooner or later.

Consider asking the following questions as you go through the interview process not only to demonstrate your professional bearing, but also to get those answers needed to determine whether the organization and position under consideration are worth pursuing.

Questions to Ask Recruiters, Headhunters, Agencies

Meetings with recruiters and agencies are screening interviews. The interviewers, if satisfied that you are a possible fit, refer you to the organization directly for an interview. The organization (the client) is given either a copy of your resume or a synopsis of your experience and qualifications prepared by the screener.

Is this a retainer or contingency assignment?

How long has the client been with you?

May I have a written description?

To whom does the position report?

Why is the position open?

How long has the position been open?

How long have you had the assignment?

What does the position pay?

Are there other pay/compensation/perquisites that I should take into consideration?

Who will be interviewing me?

What is his/her position/title/management style?

Who will make the final hiring decision?

Are there any other written materials to review before I agree to a meeting?

Questions to Ask
Potential Employers

These questions assume that this information is not a matter of public record or available to be researched.

Is the organization privately held? If yes, who owns it?

How long has the organization been in existence?

How many employees do you have?

Where are your other locations?

What are the organization's current major challenges?

Have there been any layoffs? When was the last one? Are more forthcoming?

May I have a copy of the current organization chart, employee handbook, in-house publications, job description?

Was this job posted internally? Are you also looking within the organization to fill the position?

Do you expect your recent rate of income/sales increase/decline to continue this year?

Do you feel I have the characteristics necessary to be hired and to advance in this organization?

How firm are the organization's requirements for the position?

What do you feel are the most important aspects of this position?

Who will be interviewing me? Position/title/management style?

Who will make the final hiring decision?

How soon do you want an employee in place?

When will you have to make a hiring decision?

How long have you worked here?

What do you like about this organization?

Would this position lead to other job openings?

Can I visit the department, get a tour of the facility?

Are there other ways of meeting the requirements of the position that may enhance the value of my experience/strengths?

Would you be able to share any financial information with me? Sales? Net income? Budget of the department that I would be a part of?

How does the organization regard its employees?

How many applicants have applied for this job?

How long do you think it will take until you make a decision?

What could I say or do to convince you to offer me this job?

Can I telephone you in _____ days to inquire about your decision?

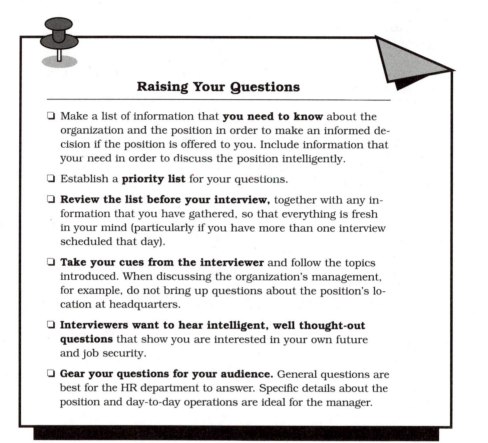

Raising Your Questions

❏ Make a list of information that **you need to know** about the
organization and the position in order to make an informed decision if the position is offered to you. Include information that
your need in order to discuss the position intelligently.

❏ Establish a **priority list** for your questions.

❏ **Review the list before your interview,** together with any information that you have gathered, so that everything is fresh
in your mind (particularly if you have more than one interview
scheduled that day).

❏ **Take your cues from the interviewer** and follow the topics
introduced. When discussing the organization's management,
for example, do not bring up questions about the position's location at headquarters.

❏ **Interviewers want to hear intelligent, well thought-out
questions** that show you are interested in your own future
and job security.

❏ **Gear your questions for your audience.** General questions are
best for the HR department to answer. Specific details about the
position and day-to-day operations are ideal for the manager.

14

Summing Up

Now What?

You have thanked the interviewer for his or her time and for all the information. You have asked and gotten answers to most of your questions. You have exchanged business cards. You have shaken hands (or not) and are now out on the street, in your car, or in a taxi. With the completion of the meeting, your work is not done. Answers are not sufficient. You need to *remember the answers* and to answer the questions not asked (*"Do I think I got the job? Will they call me back?"*).

Right after the interview, debrief yourself using the Interview Follow-up Worksheet (page 176). If you are asked back for a second meeting, you will be able to recall the details of today's meeting. If you telephone to determine whether the position has been filled (by the date they indicated), you can ask any follow-up questions about your interview or candidacy.

> *Was there anything specific in my interview or background that you felt was lacking?*
>
> *If any other comparable positions open in the near future would you be in a position to contact me?*

Additionally, in answer to another question that lingers but is never asked, send a thank you letter to address the question, *"Are you professionally courteous?"* See the Sample Thank You Letter (page 177). Refer again to your Interview Follow-Up Worksheet for any salient points of the interview that you can refer to specifically in the letter that would help the interviewer remember you.

Interview Follow-up Worksheet

After the interview, recap the following highlights:

Organization: _____

Interviewed with: _____

   Title: _____ Location: _____

How did you get this interview? _____

Was this first interview? _____ Follow-up? _____

Setting of interview: _____

Approx. how long did interview last? _____

Did it start on time? _____

Purpose of interview: _____

Position interviewed for: _____

Salary range: _____

Overall impressions of organization: _____

_____

Overall impressions of position: _____

_____

Grade yourself: what you did right or wrong _____

_____

Grade them: what they did right or wrong _____

_____

What would you do differently? _____

_____

Are you still interested in the job? _____ Why? _____

_____

Do you think they are interested in you? _____ Why? _____

_____

When will position be filled? _____

How will they follow up with you? _____

Comments: _____

_____

Sent thank you letter on _____, 19____.

Sample Thank You Letter

(On Your Letterhead)

Ms. Helen Trent
Human Resources Manager
H.G. Lippincott Manufacturing, Inc.
123 Main St.
Euclid, OH 44123

Dear Ms. Trent,

Thank you for spending time to interview me yesterday for the position of Senior Engineer—Waste Management Division. I knew that H.G. Lippincott Manufacturing, Inc. was a pioneer in sewage treatment development, but I was excited to hear about all the other environmental areas you are also currently involved in.

As promised, here is a copy of *Garbarge* magazine that contains my article on *The Myth of Recycling*. I feel that my areas of interest and expertise are a perfect mesh for the direction of your organization for the millennium, particularly with your recent successful bid to take over the recycling plant for Cleveland.

I look forward to hearing from you soon. If you have additional questions, please do not hesitate to contact me by telephone or fax.

Sincerely,

Ms. Jean Marie Janos

Enclosure

Sizing up Prospects

Whatever time you have spent finding, skimming through, deciding to buy, purchasing, and reading this book has been an investment for you that will help you to accomplish your goal of finding the job you really want.

Whether you chose to read it from cover to cover (presumably you aren't getting ready for a surprise ending) or, as we recommended at the start, to select the most beneficial sections, this book has given you valuable and new insights into job searching through the question-and-answer process of the interview itself.

The insights gained are also effective in your communication exchanges, both professionally and personally. Communication is one of life's experiences that grows in appreciation, enjoyment, challenges, and excitement, as you devote more attention and consideration to its various elements and nuances. The "art" of conversation has fallen onto hard times due to its lack of use and then, because of lack of attention (and practice), misuse. Most difficult to fathom is that the need to communicate is increasing dramatically at the same time our skills are in a precipitous free fall. It is really one of life's great ironies that our educational system, the proliferation of TV, and the general acceptance of a lower level of the ability to communicate (exacerbated by the challenges created by political diversity and multilingualism) are forces to be reckoned with at the same time the workplace is desperate for improved communication.

Sexual harassment, religious practices, disabilities, the increased inflow of non-English–speaking immigrants, telecommuting, teleconferencing, faxes, cellular phones, e-mail, the Internet, the global marketplace, even answering machines—all require increased communication skills. Technology only adds to the demands of communication. PCs that don't work, software that doesn't function, crossed telephone lines, baffling technological manuals—all demand greater communication efficiency and effectiveness.

Q and A

The greatest tools for starting, continuing, and ending a conversation are questions and answers. The questioner has the opportunity to direct the conversation. The astuteness of the answerer, in more subtle ways, determines the extent of control to be given the questioner. During the employment interview process, the more job applicants realize this important fact, the more effective they are.

The best questions are the ones that are not asked. If interviewers can get applicants to talk about topics and issues that are perhaps awkward or least desirable, they are more likely to obtain more complete and open answers.

Unaware applicants (who are perhaps not wise enough to read this book) may open up and "tell all" to persistent interviewers, blurting out opinions and information that they never planned to tell (or even thought about before being asked in the interview). Effective interviewers can lower applicants' defenses by providing an environment that makes them want to share their entire lives—the good, the bad, and *you know* whatever else!

The "New Way" to Find a Job

With good jobs decreasing and competition increasing, those who are successful in finding a job will be the ones who have an edge. Getting the leads and finding the opportunities are essential ingredients, but, once you find them, the job is still not yours. Unlike a treasure hunt, in which the map leads you directly to the treasure, the job search is loaded with steps and traps along the way. As long as interviewing continues to be the selection test of choice for most organizations in every sector of the economy, the best "interviewees" will get the jobs, not necessarily the best in other categories. Candidates must recognize that the best "products" do not always sell; a lot depends on the ad campaign, product placement in the store, and the buyer's mood. Understanding this facts helps applicants see that, although they are the best candidates, they will not get the offer because they are poor interviewees. Once you identify this opportunity, preparation for the interview becomes crucial to success. To do otherwise is to take an unnecessary gamble.

If we can expect to change careers at least three times in the course of our professional lives—not to mention the many different jobs we may have—then the skills needed to land the job that we want become increasingly important to learn and to develop on an ongoing basis. How many interviews will we need to make those three career changes?

This book has made the argument that being prepared for the job search offers a number of other benefits, including:

❑ **Improved communications skills.** Being able to carry out your end of an effective interview makes you more adept at the communication process—an increasingly demanding and valued skill.

❑ **Greater professional bearing and confidence.** If you master the interview process, you grow in confidence with the increase in your communication and conversational skills, a primary requirement for moving up the career ladder.

❑ **Heightened personal awareness.** The better you listen to yourself and others, the more adept you become at understanding yourself, your strengths, and your weaknesses. Once you recognize these, the better able you are to work on self-improvement.

❏ **Increased energy.** Instead of worrying about the next question, you find yourself thrilled to have a chance to respond.

❏ **Recognition of the art and science of interviewing as a constant learning experience.**

❏ **One more opportunity to grow and have fun with the work that you do.**

Index

About the Author

Matthew J. DeLuca is president of the Management Resource Group, Inc., a New York City–based consulting firm specializing in professional placement, training, outplacement, and other Human Resources activities for major organizations in a variety of industries. Before this he held senior HR positions for Chemical Bank and the Bank of Tokyo. Matt conducts frequent workshops on Career and Job Search efforts for several colleges, including New York University, and is invited to speak on HR topics to professional organizations throughout the United States. He is also the author of *How to Get a Job in 90 Days or Less* (McGraw-Hill), *Handbook of Compensation Management* and *Not For Profit Personnel Forms and Guidelines* (currently in its third edition).